# The Unexpected Cajun Kitchen

# The Unexpected Cajun Kitchen

## CLASSIC CUISINE WITH A TWIST OF FARM-TO-TABLE FRESHNESS

### LEIGH ANN CHATAGNIER

Skyhorse Publishing

Copyright © 2016 by Leigh Ann Chatagnier

All rights reserved. No part of this book may be reproduced in any manner without the express written consent of the publisher, except in the case of brief excerpts in critical reviews or articles. All inquiries should be addressed to Skyhorse Publishing, 307 West 36th Street, 11th Floor, New York, NY 10018.

Skyhorse Publishing books may be purchased in bulk at special discounts for sales promotion, corporate gifts, fund-raising, or educational purposes. Special editions can also be created to specifications. For details, contact the Special Sales Department, Skyhorse Publishing, 307 West 36th Street, 11th Floor, New York, NY 10018 or info@skyhorsepublishing.com.

Skyhorse® and Skyhorse Publishing® are registered trademarks of Skyhorse Publishing, Inc.®, a Delaware corporation.

Visit our website at www.skyhorsepublishing.com.

10 9 8 7 6 5 4 3 2 1

Library of Congress Cataloging-in-Publication Data is available on file.

Cover design by Laura Klynstra
Cover photographs by Leigh Ann Chatagnier

Print ISBN: 978-1-5107-1044-3
Ebook ISBN: 978-1-5107-1045-0

Printed in China

# Contents

*To my unexpected Cajun, my husband Canean, who forever changed my life for the better. This book wouldn't have been possible without your love and support, and belief in me always. Thank you for introducing me to a whole new world of food that will forever be a part of our family. I love you as big as the beach.*

# Introduction

One of my greatest pleasures in life is feeding people. Nothing satisfies me more than watching friends and family gathered around my table, eating the food I prepared, and knowing it was made with love. This is the reason I started blogging two years ago—I wanted to be able to reach more than just family and friends through food. Food is a universal language that can bring people of all races, cultures, and beliefs together with no judgement . . . just the common love of experiencing something delicious together.

I discovered this after moving to Louisiana. I was the outsider. I grew up southern, but had never eaten Cajun food, and it didn't matter! I was welcomed with open arms and asked to join in on family traditions dating back years and years. The food brought us together; well, that and the fact that I ended up marrying a Cajun. The food is what drew me in and made me fall in love with a place, its cuisine, and a culture that truly enjoys life.

I may not be a born Cajun, and I may not have grown up cooking the dishes that made Louisiana so well known, but what I do know is that after living there for a decade, the food has been an inspiration in my kitchen. By combining traditional Cajun cuisine with my own fresh, farm-to-table approach, my hope is everyone will find something in this cookbook. I want readers to get in their kitchens and make something delicious and nutritious for their families, feeling confident all the while!

Being able to share my food with more than those who sit in my kitchen is a goal I have had for some time. These dishes are made with ingredients native to Louisiana, but can be found in most grocery stores across the country (I live in Texas now), making them easy for any home cook.

Having recently had my first child, sharing my love for cooking is even more important to me. I have so many memories of being in the kitchen with my mom, and I can't wait to make new memories with my son. If just one person creates a memory with someone they love through cooking one of my dishes, then I'll be satisfied—that is what it's all about to me.

Food is love, and I have so much that I want to share. My hope for this cookbook is that it inspires people to spend a little more time eating dinner with their families and breaking bread with friends, and that it encourages you to get in the kitchen to try something new.

Cheers, from my kitchen to yours.
*Laissez le Bon Temps Roulet* (Let the Good Times Roll)

# The Essentials

# Remoulade Sauce

## Ingredients:

¼ cup celery, chopped
½ cup mayo
1 tbsp. whole grain mustard
1 tbsp. ketchup
1 tbsp. lemon juice
¼ cup scallions, chopped
1 clove garlic
1½ tsp. paprika
1 tsp. cracked black pepper
1 tsp. kosher salt
1 tbsp. worcestershire sauce
2 tbsp. horseradish
1 tbsp. fresh parsley, chopped

## Directions:

1. Combine all ingredients in a food processor and pulse until remoulade comes together, leaving the sauce slightly chunky for texture.

2. Refrigerate until ready to use and keep up to two weeks.

# Hollandaise Sauce

## Ingredients:

2 egg yolks
1 tbsp. lemon juice
2 tbsp. warm water
¼ tsp. cayenne pepper
¾ tsp. kosher salt
1 stick unsalted butter

## Directions:

1. Add 2 egg yolks to a blender along with lemon juice, half the warm water, cayenne, and salt. Blend until frothy.

2. Melt butter, careful not to brown, and gently stream the hot butter into the blender while the blender is on, until the eggs and butter have combined to make a thick sauce. Add ½ teaspoon of warm water at a time to thin out sauce.

# Fry Mix

## Ingredients:

1 cup all-purpose flour

1 tsp. salt

1 tsp. black pepper

¼ tsp. cayenne pepper

1 cup cornmeal

¼ cup milk

½ cup buttermilk

1-inch-deep vegetable oil for frying

## Directions:

1. Lay out 2 plates and one bowl.
2. On one plate, mix ½ cup of all-purpose flour with salt, pepper, and cayenne.
3. On the other plate, mix cornmeal and the remaining ½ cup of flour.
4. In a bowl, combine milk and buttermilk.
5. Dredge the ingredient you'll be frying in flour mixture, then directly place into the milk, and then dredge in the cornmeal mixture coating all sides.
6. Fry in vegetable oil until all sides are browned and cooked though.

# Simple Syrup

## Ingredients:

½ cup sugar

½ cup water

## Directions:

1. Add both ingredients to a pot and bring to a boil. Then chill thoroughly. Add to cocktails for sweetener. Will keep for 3 weeks.

# Cajun Seasoning

## Ingredients:

1 tsp. salt

1 tsp. garlic powder

1 tsp. paprika

1 tsp. black pepper

¼ tsp. cayenne pepper

1 tsp. oregano

1 tsp. thyme

½ tsp. red chili flakes

1 tsp. onion powder

1 tsp. kosher salt

## Directions:

1. Mix spices together and store in airtight container for up to a month.

**Note:** Ingredients can be doubled or tripled for a larger batch.

# Brunch

amazing !

# Pecan Praline Cinnamon Rolls

*This dish takes decadence to a whole new level, and with a hot cup of coffee, these pecan cinnamon rolls will get your weekend started right!*

## Ingredients:

### Dough

2½ cups all-purpose flour

2 tbsp. sugar

1¼ tsp. baking powder

½ tsp. baking soda

¼ tsp. salt

1¼ cups buttermilk

2 tbsp. unsalted butter, melted

### Filling

³⁄₄ cup brown sugar

¼ cup granulated sugar

2½ tsp. cinnamon

⅛ tsp. salt

4 tbsp. butter, melted

½ cup pecans, chopped

### Caramel Praline Sauce

¼ cup butter

½ cup brown sugar

½ cup heavy cream

¼ cup pecans, roughly chopped

## Directions:

1. Preheat oven to 425 degrees.

2. Combine flour, sugar, baking powder, baking soda, and salt in a bowl and whisk to combine.

3. Add buttermilk and 2 tablespoons of melted butter to the dry ingredients and stir with a wooden spoon until dough comes together. The dough should be shaggy.

4. Make the filling by combining brown sugar, granulated sugar, cinnamon, salt, 2 tablespoons melted butter, and chopped pecans until it has a wet sand-like texture.

5. Place dough onto a floured surface and knead until smooth, 1 to 2 minutes.

6. Roll the dough out into a rectangle until it's around ⅛-inch thick.

7. Brush 2 tablespoons of melted butter onto the dough and then evenly distribute the pecan cinnamon filling.

8. Carefully roll the dough until you form a log, pinching the ends to keep the log together.

9. Cut into 8 rolls and place into a greased round cake pan or cast-iron skillet.

10. To prepare caramel praline sauce, melt butter and brown sugar in a small saucepan until sugar has melted and is hot and bubbly.

11. Turn off heat and stir in heavy cream and pecans until sauce has thickened.

12. Spoon ¼ cup of the praline mixture over top of the cinnamon rolls and bake for 20 to 25 minutes until cinnamon rolls are cooked through and browned.

13. Add more praline sauce after cooking before serving. Serve immediately.

# Andouille Breakfast Pizza

## Ingredients:

### Dough

1 packet dry active yeast
1 cup warm water
2 tsp. honey
1 cup all-purpose flour
1½ cups whole wheat flour
1 tbsp. olive oil
1½ tsp. kosher salt

### Toppings

1 lb. andouille sausage
½ lb. Manchego cheese, grated
4 green onions, thinly sliced
4-5 eggs

## Directions:

1. Combine yeast, warm water, and 1 teaspoon of honey in a stand mixer.
2. Let the mixture sit for 5 to 10 minutes until yeast is bubbly.
3. Slowly add in half of both flours along with the olive oil, remaining honey, and salt, into the yeast mixture using the dough hook attachment.
4. Add in the rest of the flour at this time. Turn the mixer to medium speed and let dough come together for 5 minutes.
5. Turn dough out onto a lightly floured surface and knead a few times until a smooth ball forms. This will take about 2 to 3 minutes.
6. Place the dough in an oiled bowl and cover with a towel and leave in a warm spot to rise.
7. Let the dough rise for 30 minutes.
8. Preheat oven to 450 degrees.
9. Slice sausage into rings and sauté in a skillet on medium heat until browned. Move onto a paper towel-lined plate to remove excess grease.
10. Roll out dough on a lightly floured surface and roll out until the dough is ⅛-inch thick (or to desired thickness) and drizzle with olive oil.
11. Layer your cheese first, and then andouille sausage into a single layer.
12. Bake at 450 degrees for 15 to 20 minutes.
13. In the last 5 minutes, crack eggs over the pizza and return to the oven until whites of the eggs are cooked through.
14. Garnish with green onions and serve immediately.

# Cajun Breakfast Fried Rice

## Ingredients:

2 tbsp. sesame oil
1 tbsp. ginger, grated
2 garlic cloves, minced
¼ lb. tasso (can substitute bacon)
6 green onions, diced
3 cups cooked white rice (leftover
    rice works great)
¼ cup soy sauce
1 tbsp. rice wine vinegar
¼ cup frozen peas
4 eggs
sriracha sauce for serving

## Directions:

1. Heat 2 tablespoons of sesame oil in a large skillet or wok over medium heat.

2. Sauté ginger, garlic, Tasso, and half of the green onions until tender and Tasso has browned.

3. Add rice to the pan and fry for 5 to 10 minutes until all the flavors have combined.

4. Pour in soy sauce and rice wine vinegar and continue to stir-fry for another five minutes.

5. Add peas and heat through.

6. Melt butter in a separate skillet and fry eggs over medium-high heat until whites are cooked through.

7. Top fried rice with eggs, extra green onions, and Sriracha sauce.

# New Orleans–Style Pain Perdu

## Ingredients:

8 eggs

2 cups milk

1/3 cup sugar

¼ cup brandy

2 tsp. vanilla

1 tbsp. cinnamon

4 thick-cut slices challah bread

1 tbsp. butter

¼ cup almonds, blanched and
    sliced

maple syrup and powdered
    sugar for serving

½ cup strawberries, sliced

## Directions:

1. Combine eggs, milk, sugar, brandy, vanilla, and cinnamon in a large bowl. Mix well.

2. Pour mixture over the bread in a large bowl and let sit for 10 minutes, turning once.

3. Preheat oven to 425 degrees.

4. Heat a large skillet over medium heat, add 1 tablespoon of butter and let melt.

5. Dip your pieces of soaked bread into the almonds on one side and place almond side down on the skillet.

6. Cook for 5 to 7 minutes, turning once, and browning each side of the toast.

7. Transfer the toast to a baking sheet and continue to cook in the oven for 10 to 15 minutes until the custard is cooked through.

8. Drizzle with maple syrup and dust with powdered sugar. Serve with fresh, sliced strawberries.

# Boudin Omelette

*Boudin is a mixture of rice, meat, and spices that comes in a casing and looks like sausage. It can be found in most groceries where specialty sausages are located.*

## Potato Ingredients:

2 cups red potatoes

2 tbsp. olive oil

1 tsp. kosher salt

1 tsp. cracked pepper

1 tsp. steak seasoning

## Omelette Ingredients:

1 tbsp. celery, diced

1 tbsp. green bell pepper

1 tbsp. red bell pepper

1 tbsp. white onion

1 tbsp. olive oil + 1 tbsp. butter

4 eggs

1 tsp. black pepper

1 link of boudin sausage, casing removed

1 tsp. salt

½ cup green onions, diced

Hollandaise Sauce (see page 1)

## Directions:

1. Preheat oven to 425 degrees.
2. Slice potatoes into wedges and drizzle with 1 tbsp. of olive oil, and season with salt, pepper, and steak seasoning.
3. Roast potatoes for about 35 to 45 minutes, until potatoes are golden and crispy.
4. Sauté celery, bell peppers, and onion in 1 tablespoon of olive oil and 1 tablespoon of butter until translucent and tender, about 10 minutes. Make Hollandaise Sauce while your vegetables are sautéing.
5. Whisk two eggs at a time until yolks and whites are well combined, and season with salt and cracked pepper.
6. Heat a small skillet over medium heat and spray with nonstick spray.
7. Add eggs to the pan and let eggs set for a few minutes.
8. Layer half of the sautéed vegetables, and half of the boudin to the eggs.
9. Gently fold over one half of the omelette to cover the boudin and veggies.
10. Let cook for 2 minutes and then gently flip to cook on the other side for 2 more minutes until eggs are cooked through.
11. Repeat process one more time to make the second omelette.
12. To serve, top omelette with Hollandaise Sauce and green onions with a side of roasted potatoes.

# Shrimp and Creamy Gouda Grits

## Ingredients:

4 slices bacon

10 cups water

1 tbsp. + 1 tsp. salt

2 cups old-fashioned grits

1½ cups smoked gouda cheese, grated

2 tbsp. unsalted butter

2 tsp. cracked black pepper

3 cloves garlic, minced

2 lb. shrimp, peeled and deveined

¼ tsp. red chili flakes

¼ cup dry white wine

1 tbsp. butter

juice of 1 lemon

2 tbsp. parsley

4 green onions

## Directions:

1. Chop bacon into small pieces. Sauté bacon in a large pan until crispy. Remove from pan.

2. Bring 9 cups of water to a boil, and add 1 tablespoon of salt.

3. Whisk in grits to prevent lumps and reduce heat to simmer. Cover and let cook for 10 minutes or until grits are tender.

4. Add cheese and 2 tablespoons of butter to the grits, along with 1 teaspoon pepper, and stir until butter and cheese have melted. At this time, taste and add more salt and pepper if desired. Turn heat to low and cover.

5. Add minced garlic to bacon grease and cook for 1 minute.

6. Add shrimp in a single layer and season with salt, pepper, and red chili flakes, and cook for 2 minutes per side until shrimp are pink.

7. Remove shrimp. Add ¼ cup of wine to deglaze pan and reduce for a couple of minutes.

8. Add shrimp and bacon to the pan again and add 1 tablespoon of butter, lemon juice, and parsley.

9. Toss the shrimp with the sauce, serve over grits, and top with green onions.

# Couche Couche with Berry Maple Syrup and Cream

*Couche Couche is a traditional Louisiana cornmeal breakfast made in a skillet.*

## Ingredients:

2 cups cornmeal

1½ tsp. salt

1 tsp. baking powder

1½ cups milk

2 pieces bacon

1 cup fresh berries (any variety)

1 cup maple syrup

1 tsp. vanilla

¼ cup heavy cream

## Directions:

1. Add cornmeal, salt, baking powder, and milk, in a large bowl and mix until all ingredients are combined.

2. Sauté bacon in a cast-iron skillet until crispy and remove the bacon, leaving the drippings behind.

3. Heat the bacon drippings on medium-high heat and add the cornmeal mixture, allowing a crust to form on the bottom of the skillet, similar to making regular cornbread.

4. Reduce heat to medium and begin to scrape the pan until large lumps form and cornmeal is cooked through, about 15 to 20 minutes.

5. Chop bacon and add back to the pan.

6. Heat berries and maple syrup in a small saucepan until berries have softened and a syrup has formed.

7. Purée the berry maple syrup in a blender or food processor until smooth.

8. To serve, drizzle the berry maple syrup over the couche couche along with a drizzle of cream.

# Open-Faced Egg Sandwiches with Arugula Pesto

## Ingredients:

½ cup arugula
1 tbsp. pine nuts
1 garlic clove
¼–⅓ cup extra virgin olive oil
¼ cup parmesan cheese, grated
salt and pepper
6 strips bacon
2 eggs
2 pieces whole wheat bread
½ cup grape or cherry tomatoes, quartered

## Directions:

1. Combine arugula, pine nuts, garlic, olive oil, parmesan cheese, salt, and pepper in a food processor and blend until smooth. Set aside.

2. Cook bacon in a skillet over medium heat until crispy. Place cooked bacon onto a paper towel-lined plate to remove excess grease.

3. Heat the same pan over medium heat and crack 2 eggs over the pan in the bacon grease and fry on one side until egg whites are cooked through.

4. Toast whole wheat bread.

5. Layer 3 strips of bacon on each piece of bread, top with fried egg, and drizzle with arugula pesto.

6. Place tomatoes over top and serve immediately.

# CULTURE THROUGH FOOD

Food in Louisiana is more than just something that feeds your body. It's a tradition, a common ground, the center of any gathering, and the link to every Cajun family's ancestors. While all Cajun and Creole families might make gumbo and boil crawfish, every family has a slightly different recipe or method to cooking these traditional dishes. Their recipes have been passed down from their fathers, grandparents, or great aunts. Every time these dishes are prepared, a part of their heritage comes alive.

The pride that most Cajuns have about their cooking is something to be admired. It's one of the few cultures where both men and women alike find their way in the kitchen. The melting pot of flavors that have made Cajun cuisine what it is have people flocking to the state for a taste of the real thing! It's what made me fall in love with the culture and is one of the reasons I wanted to create this cookbook.

I love knowing my son will get to experience his Cajun heritage through the food he will learn to make—food that was passed down from his grandparents and his father and me. These core recipes—that the people in Louisiana hold dear to their hearts and still cook the way they were taught by their families—have kept the culture vibrant throughout the years.

Louisiana is one of the most culturally rooted states. The Cajun French language is still prevalent in certain areas, and the traditions are very much alive through the food that has made Louisiana famous. These traditions separate Louisiana from the rest and draw people, including me, in, making us falling in love with this place over and over again.

I believe that when visiting a new place, the best way to get to know the people and the culture is by eating the food. Through the food, you can learn so much about a place and have an instant connection with its people.

With every bite, you can taste not only the layered and intentional ingredients, but also the love poured into each dish. It's a talent that Cajun and Creole cooks have mastered and makes them unique from other areas in the country.

I had never visited Louisiana nor had I tasted any of the food that I have come to love so much today until I met my husband. Eleven years ago, I tasted my first crawfish and never looked back. I fell in love with this place, where food invited me to become a part of its culture and everything about it was authentic.

I have come to know Louisiana as my second home throughout the years of not only marrying into a Cajun family, but also through the food that I have eaten. My hope is that through my new take on traditional recipes, you will be able to experience a little bit of Louisiana in your own kitchen too.

# Cheddar Scallion Tasso Biscuit Sandwiches

## Ingredients:

2 cups self-rising flour
¼ cup cold butter, cut into pats
⅔ cup cold milk
2 scallions, chopped
1 cup cheddar cheese
1 egg, beaten well
½ lb. tasso, sliced thin
1 tbsp. mayonnaise

## Directions:

1. Preheat oven to 425 degrees.
2. Place flour in a bowl and work in the cold butter until the butter is broken up into small pieces.
3. Add your milk until the mixture just comes together.
4. Fold in scallions and cheese until well combined.
5. Scoop dough onto a well-floured surface and fold it over on itself several times until smooth. Use more flour if necessary to prevent sticking.
6. Roll the dough out into a rectangle about ½-inch thick.
7. Cut biscuits with a biscuit cutter or slice into rectangles.
8. Place biscuits onto an un-greased cookie sheet, leaving room between each biscuit.
9. Beat 1 egg and brush the top of each biscuit lightly to ensure a golden top.
10. Bake the biscuits for 10 to 15 minutes until they are golden brown.
11. While biscuits cook, sauté Tasso until browned.
12. Cut biscuits in half.
13. Spread a very thin layer of mayonnaise and then layer 1 to 2 slices of Tasso between each biscuit and serve immediately.

# Cheesy Cornmeal Waffles with Maple Bacon, Egg, and Avocado

## Ingredients:

8 slices bacon

2 tbsp. maple syrup

1³/₄ cup all-purpose flour

1¹/₄ cups yellow cornmeal

1 tbsp. baking powder

¹/₄ tsp. salt

1 cup cheddar cheese, shredded

6 eggs

1 cup milk

1 cup buttermilk

i tbsp. honey

3 tbsp. vegetable oil

1 tbsp. butter

¹/₄ tsp. red chili flakes

salt and pepper

1 avocado, sliced

## Directions:

1. Preheat oven to 400 degrees.

2. Drizzle maple syrup over bacon and place on a parchment-lined baking sheet.

3. Place bacon into the oven and let cook for 15 to 20 minutes until bacon is cooked, turning once. (Note: Keep an eye on it, as the maple syrup can burn easily.) Set bacon aside and lower oven to 200 degrees.

4. Mix flour, cornmeal, baking powder, salt, and cheese, in a bowl together and whisk to combine.

5. Combine 2 of the eggs, milk, buttermilk, honey, and oil in a small bowl and then add to the dry ingredients.

6. Heat waffle iron and cook waffles until done.

7. Keep waffles warm in a 200-degree oven until ready to serve.

8. Melt 1 tablespoon butter and fry remaining 4 eggs until whites are cooked through.

9. To serve, stack 2 waffles and then layer two pieces of maple bacon, a fried egg, and avocado over top of the waffle and sprinkle with red chili flakes. Serve immediately.

# Mini Farmers' Market Frittatas

*Any vegetables can be substituted based upon farmers' market availability!*

## Ingredients:

1 tbsp. olive oil
1 large shallot, diced
1 tbsp. sage, chopped
1 tbsp. + 1 tsp. salt
1 tsp. cracked black pepper
1 sweet potato, diced small
2 cups baby kale
8 eggs
1 tbsp. milk
1 cup mozzarella cheese
¼ cup parmesan cheese

## Directions:

1. Preheat oven to 350 degrees.
2. Line a muffin tin with individual parchment cups.
3. Heat a large skillet over medium heat and add olive oil, shallot, sage, 1 teaspoon salt, and pepper. Add sweet potatoes, sauté for 10 to 15 minutes until potatoes start to become tender, and then wilt in the kale by adding a little at a time.
4. In the meantime, in a large bowl, add eggs, 1 tablespoon milk, and the rest of the salt, and whisk until well combined.
5. Stir in mozzarella cheese.
6. Add sweet potato mixture to the eggs and stir.
7. Ladle the egg mixture into the parchment cups, about one ladle per cup.
8. Top with the parmesan cheese and bake for 20 to 25 minutes until eggs are cooked through.

# Crawfish Eggs Benedict

## Ingredients:

### *Crawfish Cake*

1 cup cooked crawfish tails

2 green onions, sliced thin

1 tbsp. fresh parsley, chopped

1 egg

1 tsp. kosher salt

½ tsp. cracked pepper

1¼ cup bread crumbs

2 tbsp. vegetable oil

### *Additional Ingredients*

4 slices canadian bacon

2 tbsp. Hollandaise Sauce
    (see page 1)

2 english muffins

2 tbsp. butter

4 eggs

1 tsp. kosher salt

2 tsp. vinegar

1 tbsp. parsley for garnish

2 tsp. vinegar

## Directions:

1. Roughly chop crawfish tails and combine with chopped green onions, parsley, egg, salt, pepper, and bread crumbs. Form 4 patties from the mixture.

2. Heat a cast-iron skillet over medium heat with vegetable oil.

3. Brown crawfish cakes on both sides for 5 minutes per side, until golden brown.

4. Sauté Canadian bacon on each side for 2 minutes in the same skillet, and remove from heat.

5. Make Hollandaise Sauce, set to the side.

6. Butter English muffins and broil until golden brown.

7. Poach eggs by heating 1 teaspoon kosher salt and 2 teaspoons of vinegar in an inch of water in a large sauce pan. Bring the water to a simmer over medium heat. Crack very cold eggs one at a time in a small ramekin and gently place into the simmering water. Turn off the heat, put the lid back on, and leave for 5 minutes with no peeking.

8. To serve, layer Canadian bacon onto English muffin, then add crawfish cake, top with poached egg, hollandaise, and garnish with green onions and parsley. Serve immediately.

# Everyday Dish

# Grilled Chicken Thighs with Smoky Whipped Sweet Potatoes

## Ingredients:

### Chicken

- 4 skin-on chicken thighs
- ¼ cup balsamic vinegar
- 2 tbsp. olive oil
- 1 tbsp. salt
- 1 tsp. cracked pepper
- 2 tbsp. parsley, chopped

### Sweet Potatoes

- 2 cups sweet potatoes, peeled and diced in large cubes
- 2 chipotle peppers in adobo sauce + 1 tsp. sauce
- ¼ cup honey
- 1½ tsp. salt
- 2 tbsp. butter
- ⅓ cup milk

## Directions:

1. Marinate chicken with balsamic vinegar, olive oil, salt, and pepper, for 30 minutes (or as long as overnight) in a plastic zip bag or airtight container.

2. Place potatoes in a large pot and cover potatoes with water.

3. Bring the potatoes to a boil. Boil until potatoes are fork tender, about 15 minutes.

4. In the meantime, preheat grill to 400 degrees.

5. Sear the chicken for 3 minutes on each side.

6. Reduce heat to 350 degrees and remove the chicken from direct heat or onto the top rack of the grill. (Can also be done on an indoor grill pan.)

7. Continue to cook until chicken is cooked through, about 20 more minutes. Remove chicken from the grill and let rest for 5 minutes.

8. With a hand-held mixer or stand mixer, whip your sweet potatoes with the chipotle peppers and their sauce, honey, salt, butter, and milk, until smooth.

9. Sprinkle the chicken with parsley and serve alongside the sweet potatoes.

# Crawfish Curry Noodle Bowl

## Ingredients:

1 green bell pepper
1 jalapeño pepper
4 green onions
2 cloves garlic
1 tbsp. ginger
1 tbsp. coconut oil
3 tbsp. curry powder
1 tbsp. water
1 lb. crawfish tails
1 can coconut milk
¼ cup fresh tomatoes,
    chopped
1 tsp. salt
1 lb. rice noodles

## Directions:

1. Chop bell pepper, jalapeño pepper, 2 of the green onions, garlic, and ginger.
2. Heat coconut oil over medium heat in a large skillet.
3. Add your chopped veggies to the pan and sauté for 5 minutes until vegetables are tender.
4. Combine curry powder and water together in a small bowl and stir to make a paste.
5. Add curry paste to the vegetables and sauté for 2 minutes.
6. Add in crawfish and coconut milk. Stir to combine and cook for 10 minutes.
7. Add in tomatoes, season with salt, and heat through for 2 more minutes.
8. In the meantime, bring a large pot of water to a boil, add rice noodles, and boil until just tender (3 to 4 minutes).
9. Drain and rinse the noodles.
10. Serve crawfish curry over noodles and top with remaining 2 diced green onions.

# Cajun Shrimp Cobb Salad with Bacon Blue Cheese Vinaigrette

## Ingredients:

### Salad

6 slices thick-cut bacon

1 lb. large shrimp, peeled and deveined

2 tbsp. Cajun Seasoning (see page 3)

1 tbsp. olive oil

1 head romaine lettuce

2 cups mixed greens

¼ cup red onion, sliced

1 tomato, chopped

1 english cucumber, chopped

2 ears fresh corn, cooked and kernels removed

1 avocado

4 hard-boiled eggs

½ cup blue cheese crumbles

### Vinaigrette

bacon drippings from the cooked bacon (about ⅓ cup)

¼ cup apple cider vinegar

⅛ cup blue cheese crumbles

3 tbsp. honey

1 tsp. cracked pepper

2 green onions, chopped

## Directions:

1. Cook bacon in a large skillet over medium heat until crispy, remove from the pan, place on a paper towel–lined plate, and set aside.

2. Season shrimp with Cajun Seasoning and heat olive oil over medium-high heat on an indoor grill pan or large skillet.

3. Add shrimp and cook about 2 minutes on each side until shrimp are just cooked through and have turned pink.

4. To make the vinaigrette, heat bacon drippings over medium heat and add vinegar, blue cheese, honey, pepper, and green onions. Cook for 5 minutes until cheese is melted and flavors have combined. Remove from heat and store in a mason jar until ready to serve. Best served hot or room temperature.

5. Layer lettuce and greens, onion, tomato, cucumber, corn, avocado, eggs, cheese, and shrimp.

6. Drizzle vinaigrette over salad when ready to serve.

# Chicken and Andouille Sausage Gumbo with Fried Okra Dippers

## Ingredients:

### *Gumbo*

2 large onions

1 cup celery

1 cup green bell pepper

½ cup green onions

1 whole chicken

4 tbsp. Cajun Seasoning
    (see page 3)

1 lb. andouille sausage

½ cup + 2 tbsp.
    vegetable oil

1 cup all-purpose flour

9 cups chicken stock

3 bay leaves

1 tbsp. kosher salt

1 tsp. black pepper

¼ cup fresh parsley

¼ tsp. cayenne

4 cups cooked white
    rice

### *Fried Okra Dippers*

½ cup vegetable oil

1 lb. fresh whole okra

Fry Mix (see page 3)

kosher salt for sprinkling

## Directions:

1. Chop onions, celery, bell pepper, and green onions.
2. Rub the chicken with Cajun Seasoning.
3. Heat 2 tablespoons of oil in a large pot and brown your chicken on all sides, but not fully cooked through. Remove chicken and set to the side to rest.
4. Sauté the sausage in the same pot and remove when browned.
5. Make the roux by adding vegetable oil and flour to the pot over medium to medium-high heat.
6. Stir the roux for 20 to 25 minutes consistently, until the roux is caramel in color, careful to watch the heat and not let the roux burn. Adjust the heat accordingly if the roux starts to brown too quickly.
7. Add the veggies to the roux and season with salt, pepper, and cayenne pepper. Cook for 5 to 10 minutes until veggies start to tenderize.
8. Add sausage back to the pot.
9. At this time, pour in chicken stock and bay leaves.
10. Add the whole chicken back to the pot to continue cooking all the way through.
11. Simmer the gumbo for 2 hours until chicken is falling apart and all flavors have combined.
12. Remove chicken and shred the meat, discarding the skin and the bones. Add chicken meat back to the gumbo.
13. About 30 minutes before gumbo is ready to serve, heat vegetable oil in a cast-iron skillet over medium heat until it reaches about 375 degrees. Test the temperature by adding a little of the Fry Mix to the oil to see if it's hot enough—it should sizzle when ready.
14. Coat okra in the Fry Mix and place the okra in the hot oil. Cook on both sides for 2 to 3 minutes until golden brown.
15. Remove okra to a paper towel-lined plate and sprinkle with kosher salt.
16. To serve gumbo, spoon over white rice with fried okra dippers on the side and sprinkle with fresh parsley.

# A FARM-FRESH SPIN

One of my favorite ways to get inspired in the kitchen is to shop at local farmers' markets. I fell in love with the idea of farmers' markets after moving to Louisiana and found myself doing most of my shopping with local farmers each week. Letting the produce and meats available dictate my menu planning each week is exciting and allows me to experiment with new takes on all my favorite recipes.

Louisiana in particular has a warmer climate throughout most of the year, allowing an abundance of produce to grow throughout the year. On top of that, I can find meats and seafood of all varieties including lamb, beef, goat, shrimp, crab, alligator, free range chickens, and pork. I call the Red Stick Farmers' Market in Baton Rouge, Louisiana, my home market. I know my farmers and they know me. I got hooked on items like Berkshire ground pork (which makes the richest and juiciest burger because it comes from a breed of pig dating back three hundred years) and fresh produce including figs, greens of all varieties, and satsumas, to name a few. Not only is there fresh produce and meats, but also homemade jams, dips, breads, and so much more.

In addition to the quality of the food at local farmers' markets being top notch, there is something about the feeling of community you get when you shop your local market. Fresh flowers, families enjoying the outdoors, seeing your neighbor while you grab a breakfast pastry, and knowing you are buying quality ingredients from farmers who need your support are all reasons that farmers' markets rank high on my list no matter where I live.

After moving to Texas, I will say that the single thing I miss most about Louisiana is my local market. I knew my farmers and looked forward to seeing them as well as friends every Saturday morning. Regardless if you have a farmers' market near you, you can find seasonal produce and quality meat at most grocery stores these days. I try to shop items grown nearby or locally when I can't shop fresh from the farm! Knowing where my food comes from is important to me, and I feel better about eating it knowing where it was produced.

In this book, you'll find that I took my favorite Louisiana recipes and showed you my own take on how I make them in my kitchen, which in most cases includes farm-fresh ingredients. These somewhat fresher takes on the classics are Cajun-approved and I think you will love creating them wherever you live!

Check out the local markets in your area and see what is available. Try something new and get to know the farmers and people who live in your community. You can find almost all of the ingredients used in this book throughout the country and, more times than not, can substitute seasonal ingredients as they are available. My hope is that you can experience a little taste of the food that I have grown to love so much by cooking a fresher take on Cajun cuisine in your own kitchen!

# Seafood Pastalaya

## Ingredients:

1 onion

½ cup celery

1 green bell pepper

1 tbsp. butter

1 tbsp. olive oil

2 cloves garlic

1 can diced tomatoes

1 cup chicken broth

1 tbsp. Cajun Seasoning (see
   page 3)

1 dozen large shrimp, peeled
   and deveined

1 dozen littleneck clams

1 dozen mussels

1 lb. crabmeat

1 tbsp. kosher salt

1 lb. spaghetti pasta noodles

1 tsp. cracked black pepper

4 green onions for topping

2 tbsp. fresh parsley,
   chopped

## Directions:

1. Chop onion, celery, and bell pepper.

2. Heat butter and olive oil over medium heat in a large and deep skillet.

3. Add onion, bell pepper, celery, and garlic to the pan and cook for 5 minutes until vegetable are tender. Season with salt and pepper.

4. Add can of tomatoes, chicken broth, and Cajun Seasoning, and let cook for another 5 minutes.

5. Add seafood and cover the skillet. Let the seafood cook for 5 minutes until clams and mussels open and shrimp are cooked through.

6. Meanwhile, bring a large pot of water to a boil. Heavily salt the water and add pasta and cook until al dente, according to the package instructions.

7. Drain the pasta, reserving ¼ cup of pasta water.

8. Add pasta into the seafood mixture along with the reserved pasta water.

9. Top with green onions and parsley and serve immediately.

# Crawfish Butternut Squash Mac N' Cheese

*Everyone loves mac n' cheese, and with my creamy butternut squash cheese sauce and spicy crawfish thrown in for a twist on a favorite, your whole family is sure to love this dish!*

## Ingredients:

1 butternut squash
1 tbsp. olive oil
1 tsp. kosher salt
2 tsp. black pepper
1 lb. pasta shells
4 tbsp. flour
4 tbsp. butter
1 cup milk
1 pinch nutmeg
1 cup pecorino romano
    cheese
1 lb. crawfish tails
½ cup plain bread
    crumbs
2 tbsp. parsley

## Directions:

1. Preheat oven to 425 degrees.

2. Cut the butternut squash in half, peel, remove the seeds, and then cut into large, 1-inch chunks.

3. Layer squash onto a baking sheet and add olive oil, salt, and half the pepper, and toss to coat.

4. Bake for 35 to 45 minutes until squash is caramelized and tender.

5. Bring water to a boil in a large pot. Heavily salt the water and then add pasta shells and cook until just before al dente. (They will finish cooking in the oven.) Drain the pasta, reserving ¼ cup of pasta water.

6. Purée your squash after it cools slightly, adding the reserved pasta water to thin out the squash purée.

7. In a medium-sized pot, add flour and butter and cook for a couple minutes until the roux has cooked a bit. Slowly add in the milk, whisking the whole time to prevent lumps.

8. Season the béchamel with salt, pepper, and nutmeg, and let thicken for 5 to 10 minutes until the mixture coats the back of a wooden spoon.

9. Add the butternut squash purée to the béchamel sauce along with half of the Pecorino Romano cheese and stir until cheese has melted and butternut squash is combined.

10. Add crawfish tails and heat through.

11. Pour pasta shells into the cheesy butternut squash sauce and place in greased ramekins or baking dish.

12. Combine the rest of the cheese with the bread crumbs and parsley and sprinkle liberally over the mac n' cheese to create a crust.

13. Drizzle the crust with olive oil and bake for 20 to 25 minutes until bubbly and brown. Serve immediately.

# Shrimp Po' Boy

## Ingredients:

1 lb. large shrimp, peeled and
    deveined
1 tbsp. kosher salt
1 tsp. black pepper
Fry Mix (see page 3)
½ cup vegetable oil
½ cup Remoulade Sauce (see
    page 1)
4 pieces lettuce
4 tomato slices
4 french bread rolls

## Directions:

1. Season shrimp with salt and pepper.
2. Dredge the shrimp in the Fry Mix.
3. Heat oil in a cast-iron skillet over medium-high heat until heat reaches 375 degrees, or test by placing some Fry Mix into the hot oil—if it sizzles, it's hot enough.
4. Cook shrimp on each side 2 to 3 minutes, until golden brown and cooked through.
5. Place the cooked shrimp on a paper towel-lined plate to rid of excess grease.
6. Slather Remoulade Sauce on both sides of the French bread and layer shrimp, lettuce, and tomato in between.
7. Serve immediately.

# Catfish Tacos with Tasso White Beans

*These tacos are Louisiana-fied with pan fried catfish and savory white beans seasoned with tasso ham and topped with crunchy cabbage to create the perfect taco combination!*

## Ingredients:

½ lb. white beans

1 tbsp. olive oil

1 onion, diced

1 jalapeño, diced

2 garlic cloves, minced

½ lb. tasso

4-6 cups chicken stock

4 catfish filets, cut into thin
    strips

Fry Mix (see page 3)

½ cup vegetable oil

½ cup purple cabbage

juice from 1 lime

1 tbsp. kosher salt

1 tsp. black pepper

1 avocado, sliced

¼ cup cilantro, chopped

flour or corn tortillas

## Directions:

1. Soak white beans overnight in water.

2. Heat olive oil over medium heat in a large pot. Sauté onion, jalapeño, and garlic in the olive oil until tender.

3. Add in Tasso, beans, and 4 cups of chicken stock. Add more chicken stock as the beans cook if liquid evaporates.

4. Cook for 4 to 6 hours until the Tasso is pull-apart tender and beans are cooked through. (Can be made in advance or in a crock pot.)

5. Dredge catfish strips in the Fry Mix. Heat vegetable oil in a large skillet over medium-high heat until the temperature reaches 375 degrees.

6. Cook catfish on both sides for 3 to 5 minutes until fish is cooked through and batter is golden.

7. Place the cooked catfish on a paper towel-lined plate to rid of excess grease. Shred cabbage and squeeze lime juice over cabbage and toss with salt and pepper, let sit 10 minutes.

8. Warm tortillas in the oven.

9. To prepare tacos, layer catfish, white beans, cabbage, avocado, cilantro, and serve immediately.

# Healthy Shrimp and Corn Chowder

## Ingredients:

3 stalks celery, diced, with leaves included

1 onion, diced

1 tbsp. extra virgin olive oil

1 tbsp. butter

3 russet potatoes, peeled and diced

5 sprigs fresh thyme

4 cups chicken stock

⅛ cup clam juice

2 tbsp. salt

2 tsp. pepper

1 cup milk, fat-free or 2%

1 lb. of shrimp, peeled

2 cups frozen or fresh corn kernels

green onions for topping

## Directions:

1. In a large pan, sauté the celery and onion in the olive oil and butter on medium heat until they start to soften.

2. Add the potatoes, thyme, chicken stock, clam juice, salt, and pepper. Bring to a boil.

3. Reduce heat to a simmer and continue to cook until potatoes are cooked through, about 15 minutes.

4. Add the milk and bring the broth back up to a simmer and then add shrimp and corn and cook until shrimp are pink and corn is warmed through.

5. Taste the broth to see if more salt or pepper is needed at this time.

6. Serve with crusty bread or saltines and chop some green onions for garnish.

# Shrimp, Andouille, and Okra Stew

## Ingredients:

1 lb. andouille Sausage, sliced
   into thin discs
1 cup fresh okra, diced
2 garlic cloves
2 bay leaves
3 green onions, chopped
1 tsp. red pepper flakes
1 lb. shrimp, peeled and
   deveined
salt and pepper to taste
1 can diced tomatoes, juice
   included
salt and pepper to taste

## Directions:

1. Heat a large pot over medium heat and brown the sausage until it starts to get color on both sides.

2. Add the okra, garlic, bay leaves, one chopped green onion, and red pepper flakes and sauté until the okra loses some of its strings (they will naturally fall out) and garlic softens.

3. Add the shrimp and salt and pepper to season. Stir until shrimp are just pink.

4. Add can of tomatoes, another sprinkle of salt and pepper, and stir. Cover and let simmer for 15 minutes.

5. Before serving, top with the remaining green onions and serve over rice in a bowl.

# Fried Green Tomato BLTs with Caramelized Onion Remoulade

## Ingredients:

1 lb. thick-cut bacon

2 onions, sliced

1 tbsp. olive oil

½ cup nonfat Greek yogurt

1 tbsp. reduced fat olive oil mayo

salt and pepper to taste

2 green tomatoes

Fry Mix (see page 3)

1 cup mixed greens

4 slices white bread

## Directions:

1. Place bacon on an aluminum foil-lined baking sheet.

2. Set oven to 400 degrees.

3. Place bacon in the oven before the oven is actually preheated and, as the oven comes to full temp, the bacon will cook slowly.

4. Cook the bacon for 20 to 25 minutes until crispy, turning once.

5. While bacon is cooking, slice onions and cook over medium-low heat with the olive oil until the onions are lightly browned and caramelized.

6. After they have cooled slightly, add the onions to the food processor along with Greek yogurt, mayo, salt, and pepper. Pulse until thoroughly combined. Set aside.

7. After bacon is done, place it on a paper towel-lined plate to drain any excess grease.

8. Slice tomatoes into about ¼-inch-thick slices. Dredge each slice in the Fry Mix.

9. Heat vegetable oil in a cast-iron skillet over medium-high heat and fry the tomatoes on each side for 2 to 3 minutes, until golden brown.

10. Toast bread until golden brown.

11. Spread a layer of the caramelized onion mayo on each piece of bread, and then layer mixed greens, bacon, and tomato. Serve immediately.

# Cajun Spiced Pork Burgers

## Ingredients:

2 lb. ground pork

2 tbsp. Cajun Seasoning (see page 3)

½ cup Remoulade Sauce (see page 1)

6 slices white cheddar cheese

6 brioche buns

1 tbsp. salted butter

6 pieces romaine or leaf lettuce

6 slices red onion

## Directions:

1. Heat grill to 400 degrees or indoor grill pan to medium-high heat.

2. Combine the pork and Cajun Seasoning and form 6 burger patties.

3. Make Remoulade Sauce and set aside.

4. Grill burgers on each side for 5 to 7 minutes until cooked through, leaving the grill lid open while the burgers cook.

5. Place cheese on each burger and close the grill lid until cheese is melted, another 2 minutes.

6. On a griddle or large pan, melt salted butter and place the buns cut-side down to toast slightly until browned on the inside, or alternatively place on the grill until buns have toasted.

7. To plate, layer remoulade on both sides of the bun and then top with onion, lettuce, and the pork burger. Serve immediately.

# Date Night

# New Orleans–Style BBQ Shrimp

## Ingredients:

1 tbsp. olive oil
1/4 cup onion, chopped
2 garlic cloves, minced
salt and pepper to taste
2 tbsp. Cajun Seasoning (see page 3)
1/4 cup white wine
1/4 cup fresh lemon juice, about 2 lemons
2 bay leaves
½ cup worcestershire sauce
½ cup unsalted butter
11/2 lb. large gulf shrimp, unpeeled
¼ cup chives, chopped
french bread for dipping

## Directions:

1. Heat olive oil over medium heat in a large skillet.

2. Add onion, garlic, salt, and pepper, and let cook for 2 to 3 minutes.

3. Add Cajun spice and continue to cook for 2 to 3 more minutes.

4. Deglaze the pan by adding the wine and lemon juice, and cook for another couple of minutes until wine reduces.

5. Add bay leaves and Worcestershire sauce and stir to combine. Let reduce for 5 minutes, and then add butter to the pan.

6. Continue to reduce and thicken sauce for another 5 to 10 minutes.

7. Add shrimp to the pan and let cook until pink, about 3 to 5 minutes, stirring to coat shrimp with sauce.

8. Serve shrimp in a bowl with a generous amount of sauce, topped with chives, and French bread on the side for dipping.

# A SPICY REVOLUTION

Close your eyes. You're in South Louisiana and it's the heat of summer. The humidity is at an all-time high and the aromas of various spices are wafting through your nose. The sun is out strong and right now you'd do just about anything for a cold beer.

Someone is boiling crawfish nearby. Hot and spicy crawfish. Seems like a strange thing to enjoy when your body is already radiating heat, although oddly enough, the two go hand-in-hand. My first memory of a crawfish boil goes something like this . . .

The whole family has gathered 'round, people are chatting (some in Cajun French, which I can't understand but love all the same), the heat is relentless as everyone gathers under a small section of shade. There's a long picnic table and rolls of paper towels are placed periodically down the center. My father-in-law, who happens to be the best boiler I've ever met, announces the crawfish are ready and we all scurry quickly to claim our spot at the table. The crawfish are poured out directly onto the table piping hot and I grab my first, unsure of what to do next. I follow instructions given to me by family members, and although I'm a little slower than the rest, I am immediately hooked on these spicy little crustaceans. It didn't take me long to get the hang of the whole thing, and these days I can keep up with most born Cajuns when it comes to peeling and eating crawfish.

There is just something about a hot Louisiana day that is more satisfying when your mouth is tingling from deliciously boiled crawfish. That, followed by drinking an ice-cold beer, is the perfect Saturday in my book. It's this spicy quality in Cajun cuisine that I love so much. I have always been a fan of spicy foods of all varieties, and my enjoyment for a little heat grew to an all-time high after living in Louisiana. The good news is, the spiciness does not stop with crawfish boils. Traditional Cajun seasoning is found in most of the traditional dishes prepared.

You can buy several brands of premade Cajun seasoning in stores, but I prefer making my own since usually most of the spices are already in my spice cabinet. I share my own Cajun seasoning in this book; to me it is just the right balance of heat!

In most cultures where spicy food is prevalent, rice is usually served as part of the core diet—the same is true in Louisiana. Rice has always been a staple in Cajun cuisine, and it's no wonder since it's the perfect side to serve alongside spicy dishes. Grown locally, rice has always been easily accessible and can be eaten during breakfast, lunch, or dinner. My husband was raised eating eggs and rice for breakfast, which is what inspired my Cajun Breakfast Fried Rice on page 10.

Louisiana as a whole has a spicy culture, so it only makes sense that the food would reflect this. The spice is not for the faint of heart, but even when your lips are burning, the food and taste of this place is something to be remembered.

# Easy Roasted Salmon over Corn Maque Choux

## Ingredients:

### *Corn Maque Choux*

6 ears corn

2 tbsp. butter

1 tbsp. olive oil

1 red bell pepper

1 onion

4 green onions

1/2 tsp. paprika

2 sprigs fresh thyme

2 tsp. kosher salt

1 tsp. black pepper

$\frac{1}{2}$ cup heavy cream

$\frac{1}{4}$ tsp. cayenne

$\frac{1}{4}$ cup fresh parsley,
    chopped

### *Salmon*

$\frac{3}{4}$ lb. wild sockeye salmon

1 tbsp. kosher salt

1$\frac{1}{2}$ tsp. cracked black
    pepper

1 tbsp. fresh lemon juice

1 tbsp. fresh parsley,
    chopped

## Directions:

1. Preheat oven to 425 degrees.

2. Remove corn kernels from the corn cobs.

3. Heat a skillet over medium high heat; add butter and olive oil.

4. Add red bell pepper, onion, green onions, paprika, thyme, salt, and pepper. Cook for 5 minutes.

5. Add corn and cook for another 2 minutes.

6. At this time, add heavy cream and let simmer for 5 minutes. Top with fresh parsley.

7. Season salmon with salt and pepper and place on an aluminum foil-lined baking sheet.

8. Cook the salmon for 12 minutes, turning the oven to broil for the last 2 minutes.

9. Squeeze fresh lemon juice over top of the salmon and sprinkle with parsley before serving.

10. Serve salmon alongside or over top of the corn maque choux.

# Tasso, Pear, and Brie Pizza

*In my book, nothing says "I love you" more than a homemade pizza—this combination of savory tasso ham, creamy brie, and sweet pear will be your new favorite Friday night in.*

## Ingredients:

1 cup warm water
1 packet dry yeast
4 tsp. honey
1 tbsp. + 2 tsp. olive oil
1½ tsp. kosher salt
2½–2¾ cups all-purpose flour
½ lb. tasso
2 red pears
¾ lb. brie
1 large shallot
fresh cracked black pepper

## Directions:

1. Combine yeast, warm water, and 1 teaspoon of honey in a stand mixer.

2. Let sit for 5 minutes until yeast is bubbly.

3. Add in olive oil, another teaspoon of honey, salt, and half of the flour, and mix on medium speed with a dough hook.

4. Slowly add the rest of the flour and knead until a dough ball has formed, about 5 minutes.

5. Turn out dough onto a heavily floured surface and knead by hand for 2 to 3 minutes until dough is smooth.

6. Place into an oiled bowl, cover with a dish towel, and let rise for 30 minutes in a warm place.

7. After the dough has risen for 30 minutes, turn out onto a floured and clean surface.

8. Preheat oven to 450 degrees.

9. Slice brie, Tasso, pear, and shallot, into very thin slices.

10. Punch dough down and divide the dough into two equal halves.

11. Knead each half for 2 minutes until you have a smooth ball.

12. Roll out the dough to about ⅛-inch thick.

13. Drizzle with 1 teaspoon of olive oil, and top with sliced brie, thinly sliced Tasso, pear, and shallots.

14. Crack fresh black pepper over top before putting into the oven for 20 minutes.

15. Remove from oven and drizzle each pizza with 1 teaspoon of honey.

# Cajun Spiced Sea Scallop Caesar Salad

## Ingredients:

2 tbsp. olive oil

1 cup day-old bread, diced into large cubes

½ cup parmesan cheese

12 sea scallops

2 tbsp. Cajun Seasoning (see page 3)

2 tbsp. butter

2 romaine lettuce hearts

½ tsp. salt

½ tsp. cracked pepper

### *Caesar Dressing*

¼ cup mayonnaise

2 tbsp. dijon mustard

½ tsp. worcestershire sauce

1 tsp. anchovy paste

1 garlic clove

juice of 1 lemon

pinch salt

black pepper to taste

## Directions:

1. Preheat oven to 350 degrees.

2. Drizzle olive oil over bread cubes and sprinkle with salt and pepper. Toss to combine.

3. Spread out bread evenly onto a baking sheet and bake for 5 minutes and then switch oven to broil for about 1 minute to brown the tops of the croutons, careful not to burn.

4. Make dressing by combining mayo, Dijon mustard, Worcestershire sauce, anchovy paste, garlic, lemon juice, salt, and pepper, in a food processor and blend until well combined. Set aside.

5. To make the cheese wheels, grate parmesan cheese onto a silpat or parchment-lined baking sheet into 6 piles, about a tablespoon each.

6. Bake at 350 degrees until cheese has melted, about 3 to 5 minutes. Let cool and set aside.

7. Pat scallops dry on both sides to ensure a good sear. Season both sides of the scallops with the Cajun Seasoning.

8. Heat an iron skillet over medium-high heat and add 2 tablespoons of butter.

9. Sear scallops on each side for 3 minutes, until crust has formed and scallops are done cooking.

10. Arrange romaine lettuce onto two plates, add scallops, cheese wheels, and croutons, and drizzle dressing over top. Serve immediately.

# Chicory Coffee Rubbed NY Strips and Skillet Haricot Verts

## Ingredients:

### Steaks

- 2 tbsp. ground chicory coffee
- 2 tbsp. brown sugar
- 1 tbsp. chili powder
- 2 tsp. kosher salt
- 1 tsp. paprika
- 1 tsp. cracked black pepper
- 1 tsp. dry mustard
- 2 (1½ inch thick) new york strip steaks

### Haricot Verts

- 1 lb. Haricot Verts (French Green Beans)
- 1 Shallot
- 1 Garlic Clove, minced
- ¼ cup Chicken Stock
- 1 tsp. Kosher Salt
- 1 tsp. Black Pepper

## Directions:

1. Combine coffee, brown sugar, chili powder, kosher salt, paprika, black pepper, and dry mustard in a small bowl to make a rub.

2. Bring steaks to room temperature and rub them liberally with the coffee spice blend.

3. Heat grill to high heat, about 500 degrees.

4. On the stove, bring a large pot of water to a boil.

5. Add green beans and cook for two minutes.

6. Remove the green beans and immediately shock in ice-cold water. Drain thoroughly.

7. In a large skillet, heat olive oil over medium heat. Sauté shallot and garlic for 2 to 3 minutes until tender, careful not to burn.

8. Add in blanched green beans, chicken stock, salt, and pepper, and sauté for 5 minutes or until chicken stock has reduced.

9. Cook steaks on the grill with lid open for 5 minutes per side.

10. Let rest after removing from the heat for 5 minutes until ready to serve.

11. Serve alongside haricot verts.

# Satsuma Chipotle Roasted Chicken with a Citrus Pecan Salad

*Simple meals that are fresh and full of flavor happen to be one of my favorite ways to cook. This roasted chicken with a fresh salad is the perfect way to wow that special someone and to utilize the ingredients found at your local farmers' market.*

## Ingredients:

### Chicken

½ cup fresh satsuma juice (can substitute another citrus fruit)

3 tbsp. fresh rosemary

3 chipotle peppers in adobo sauce + 1 tbsp. sauce

2 garlic cloves

1 tbsp. kosher salt

1 tsp. cracked black pepper

1 whole chicken

### Citrus Pecan Salad

3 cups mixed greens

¼ cup whole pecans

2 oz. crumbled goat cheese

1 grapefruit, peeled and sliced

1 orange, peeled and sliced

### Vinaigrette

2 tbsp. dijon mustard

1 tsp. honey

¼ cup red wine vinegar

¼ cup extra virgin olive oil

1 tsp. kosher salt

1 tsp. cracked pepper

## Directions:

1. Mix satsuma juice, rosemary, chipotle peppers and sauce, garlic, salt, and pepper, in a food processor and pulse until well combined.

2. Pour over the chicken and let sit for 2 hours (or overnight).

3. Preheat oven to 425 degrees.

4. Place chicken in a Dutch oven and cover for 40 minutes.

5. After 40 minutes, remove the lid and cook for 15 to 20 more minutes until skin has browned nicely and chicken is cooked through.

6. Loosely tent the chicken with aluminum foil and let the chicken rest for 10 minutes before serving.

7. For the salad, combine the greens, pecans, goat cheese, and citrus slices in a bowl and drizzle dressing on top.

8. Combine Dijon mustard, honey, red wine vinegar, olive oil, salt, and pepper in a small bowl and whisk to combine to make dressing.

9. Dress the salad right before serving. Serve chicken alongside salad.

# Blackened Redfish over Garlic Spinach and Cheesy Polenta

## Ingredients:

### *Redfish*

2 redfish filets

2 tbsp. Cajun Seasoning
   (see page 3)

¼ cup unsalted butter

2 links boudin

### *Spinach*

1 tbsp. olive oil

2 garlic cloves

1 lb. spinach

### *Polenta*

1³/₄ cup cornmeal

6 cups water

1 tbsp. salt

1³/₄ cup cornmeal

4 tbsp. unsalted butter

½ cup parmesan cheese

½ tsp. cracked black
   pepper

## Directions:

1. Season redfish with Cajun Seasoning on both sides.

2. Melt butter in an iron skillet over high heat.

3. Add fish to the hot pan and cook on each side for 5 to 6 minutes, until fish is flaky.

4. Meanwhile, heat boudin through on a grill pan or skillet.

5. Remove boudin from casing and top the fish, one link per piece of fish.

6. In a large skillet, heat olive oil over medium heat.

7. Add garlic to the oil and immediately start adding spinach, wilting a little at a time.

8. Cook until spinach is just wilted and garlic is fragrant, about 5 minutes.

9. Bring water to a boil in a large pot and add salt once the water is boiling.

10. Whisk in cornmeal to ensure the polenta will be smooth.

11. Reduce the heat, cover, and simmer for 15 minutes until the polenta is thick and creamy.

12. Stir in butter and cheese until melted and creamy.

13. Taste, and adjust salt and pepper as needed.

*To serve, spoon some polenta onto a plate topped with spinach, followed by the redfish and boudin.

## Ingredients:

1 lb. crawfish tails
2 tbsp. olive oil
2 garlic cloves, minced
1 tbsp. fresh parsley
1 tsp. salt
½ tsp. pepper
15 oz. ricotta cheese
50–60 wonton wrappers
¼ cup water
¼ tsp. red pepper flakes
1 can crushed tomatoes
½ cup dry white wine
½ cup heavy whipping
    cream
½ cup parmesan cheese
¼ cup clam juice

# Crawfish Ravioli

## Directions:

1. Roughly chop crawfish tails.
2. Heat 1 tablespoon of olive oil over medium heat in a large skillet.
3. Add 1 clove of minced garlic, crawfish tails, parsley, and salt and pepper to the pan and sauté until garlic is tender and crawfish have heated through.
4. Remove from heat and add crawfish mixture to a bowl along with the ricotta cheese.
5. To prepare wonton wrappers, cut out circles with a biscuit or cookie cutter.
6. Lay out circles onto a parchment-lined baking sheet and place a teaspoon of the crawfish filling in the center of each circle, careful not to overfill.
7. Brush the edge of the wonton wrapper with water, place the top circle on, and press to seal the ravioli. Use a fork to create a decorative edge and ensure seal. Continue same steps with the rest of the wonton wrappers.
8. In the same skillet that crawfish were heated in, add another tablespoon of olive oil and sauté the rest of the garlic with the red pepper flakes.
9. Add in crushed tomatoes, wine, salt, and pepper, and stir to combine. Continue to cook for another 5 minutes.
10. In the meantime, bring a large pot of water to a boil. Add a good amount of salt to the boiling water.
11. Add ravioli to the boiling water in small batches (about 6 ravioli at a time) and boil until the ravioli float. This will take about 2 to 3 minutes per batch.
12. Remove the cooked ravioli back to the parchment-lined baking sheet.
13. Turn off the heat on the tomato sauce. Add heavy cream and stir.
14. Fold in ravioli gently.
15. Top with parmesan cheese and chopped parsley and serve immediately.

# Jambalaya Pot Pies for Two

*I love the idea of taking a dish that is usually meant to feed a crowd and turning it into something more intimate. These pot pies will not disappoint and make for a perfect date night in!*

## Ingredients:

1 boneless chicken
    breast
1 link andouille
    sausage
1 boneless pork chop
2 stalks celery
1 onion
1 green bell pepper
2 cloves garlic
salt and pepper to
    taste
1 tbsp. Cajun Seasoning
    (see page 3)
2 tbsp. vegetable oil
½ cup dark beer
1 cup chicken stock
3 tbsp. flour
½ cup milk
1 tbsp. butter
1 tbsp. thyme
2 sheets puff pastry
    (thawed)
1 egg + 1 tsp. water

## Directions:

1. Dice chicken, sausage, and pork into bite-sized cubes and season with salt and pepper.
2. Chop celery, onion, bell pepper, and garlic.
3. Heat 1 tablespoon of oil in a large skillet over medium-high heat.
4. Brown all the meat in batches, careful not to overcrowd the pan to ensure good color is achieved.
5. Remove the meat from the pan once browned (it won't be cooked all the way through), and add in all chopped vegetables.
6. Season the veggies with salt, pepper, and Cajun Seasoning, and continue to sauté for 5 minutes until softened.
7. Deglaze the pan with the dark beer and let reduce for 2 minutes.
8. Add chicken stock and meat back to the pan and cover for 15 minutes to finish cooking the meat.
9. Remove meat and veggies from the liquid with a slotted spoon.
10. Make a slurry with flour and milk by combining in a mason jar and shaking vigorously until there are no lumps.
11. Add the slurry to the broth and stir until thickened. Add 1 tablespoon of butter.
12. Combine the meat and veggies back into the sauce and stir to combine.
13. Grease two individual baking dishes or one larger size baking dish and fill with the pot pie filling.
14. Top with puff pastry and trim edges with a knife, creating a slit in the middle on the top to allow steam to escape.
15. Beat 1 egg with 1 teaspoon of water to create an egg wash.
16. Brush tops with egg wash and bake for 15 to 20 minutes until tops are golden brown.

# Grilled Cajun Stuffed Pork Chops over Goat Cheese and Chive Mashed Potatoes

## Ingredients:

### Stuffed Pork Chops

1 stalk celery

½ onion

½ green bell pepper

2 garlic cloves

¼ apple

1 link andouille sausage

2 tbsp. olive oil

3 tsp. kosher salt

2 tsp. cracked black pepper

¼ cup plain bread crumbs

¼–½ cup chicken stock

1 tbsp. worcestershire sauce

2 bone-in, 2-inch-thick pork
    chops

### Mashed Potatoes

2 russet potatoes

2 tbsp. butter

2 oz. goat cheese

1 tbsp. chives, chopped

1 tbsp. salt

½ tbsp. pepper

## Directions:

1. Chop celery, onion, bell pepper, garlic, and apple, into a fine dice.

2. Chop andouille sausage into small cubes.

3. Heat 1 tablespoon olive oil in a large skillet over medium heat. Add sausage and sauté until browned.

4. Add vegetables along with 1 teaspoon salt and 1 teaspoon pepper to the sausage and continue to sauté another 5 minutes until veggies are tender.

5. Add bread crumbs and chicken stock and stir until stuffing comes together, adjusting chicken stock so stuffing is moist but not wet.

6. Season both sides of the pork chops with 1 teaspoon salt and ½ teaspoon pepper and drizzle with olive oil and Worcestershire sauce.

7. Cut a slit in the middle of the pork chop, without going all the way through, to create a pocket; spoon the stuffing inside.

8. Secure the stuffing with a toothpick on each pork chop.

9. Preheat grill to 400 degrees.

10. Grill each stuffed pork chop for 6 to 7 minutes per side until cooked through. Let rest for 5 minutes before serving.

11. Peel and dice 2 russet potatoes.

12. Place potatoes in a large pot and just cover with cold water.

13. Bring the potatoes to a boil and let simmer for about 15 minutes until potatoes are fork tender.

14. Drain the potatoes and return to the hot pot.

15. Add butter, goat cheese, chives, salt, and pepper, and whip with an electric mixer until smooth and creamy.

16. Serve pork chops alongside potatoes.

# Garlic and Herb Mussels

## Ingredients:

2 lbs. fresh mussels

2 tbsp. olive oil

2 tbsp. butter

1 large onion, diced

5 cloves garlic, minced

1 tsp. red chili flakes

salt and pepper

1 cup dry white wine

1 cup water

1 cup fresh tomatoes, diced

$\frac{1}{4}$ cup fresh basil

$\frac{1}{4}$ cup fresh parsley

baguette for dipping

## Directions:

1. To prepare mussels, scrub them with a brush to remove any dirt or grit. Then remove the beard from one side of the mussel. Simply pull on the little bits of "hair" coming out between the shell and it will come off easily. Discard any mussels that are opened and will not close back, as these are dead. Keep mussels on ice until ready to cook.

2. In a large pot, heat 1 tablespoon of olive oil, and 1 tablespoon of butter over medium heat.

3. Add onion, garlic, red chili flakes, and a good sprinkle of salt and pepper.

4. Sauté for about 5 minutes until onions become translucent.

5. Pour in white wine at this point, and bring liquid up to a simmer.

6. Let the wine reduce to half while stirring and scraping up any bits that have formed on the bottom of the pan, and then pour in water.

7. Season again with salt and pepper. Bring liquid to a boil.

8. Add mussels and put a tight-fitting lid on the pot.

9. Reduce heat to a simmer and cook for about 2 to 3 minutes until mussel shells open.

10. Add tomatoes, basil, and parsley, and stir to heat through.

11. Serve immediately with grilled crusty bread.

# Small Bites

# Black Bean Hummus

## Ingredients:

1 (13-oz. can) black beans,
    drained and rinsed
1 tbsp. cumin
1 clove garlic
2 tbsp. fresh lime juice
2 tbsp. cilantro, chopped
1 tsp. kosher salt
1 tsp. cracked black pepper
1 tbsp. tahini
¼–½ cup olive oil
vegetables for dipping
pita chips for dipping

## Directions:

1. Combine black beans, cumin, garlic, lime juice, cilantro, tahini, olive oil, salt, and pepper in a food processor and combine until smooth and creamy, starting with ¼ cup of olive oil and adding more if needed for consistency.

2. Refrigerate and serve with assorted vegetables and pita chips.

# Mini Crab Cakes with Spicy Garlic Dipping Sauce

*Makes 12 to 14 crab cakes.*

## Ingredients:

16 oz. lump crab meat
1 tbsp. mayonnaise
2 tbsp. dijon mustard
½ cup bread crumbs
1 egg
1 tsp. worcestershire
    sauce
1 tsp. old bay
½ tsp. salt
½ tsp. black pepper
¼ tsp. cayenne pepper
juice from 1 lemon

2 tbsp. butter
2 green onions, thinly
    sliced
1 tbsp. fresh parsley,
    chopped

### Dipping Sauce

2 tsp. sriracha sauce
¼ cup mayonnaise
1 garlic clove, grated

## Directions:

1. Combine Sriracha sauce, mayo, and grated garlic in a small bowl and set aside.

2. Combine crab meat, mayo, Dijon mustard, bread crumbs, egg, Worcestershire sauce, Old Bay, salt, pepper, cayenne, and lemon juice in a bowl and then form small crab cakes.

3. Heat a large nonstick skillet over medium heat and melt 2 tablespoons butter.

4. Add crab cakes and cook 4 to 5 minutes per side until golden brown on both sides.

5. Serve with extra green onions and dipping sauce.

# Garlicky Goat Cheese and Chive Spread

**Ingredients:**

4 oz. goat cheese

8 oz. cream cheese

2½ tbsp. chives, chopped

1 clove garlic, grated

1 tsp. salt

1 tsp. cracked black pepper

crackers for serving

**Directions:**

1. Bring goat cheese and cream cheese to room temperature.

2. Combine goat cheese, cream cheese, chives, garlic, salt, and pepper in a bowl and mix until smooth and creamy.

3. Serve with assorted crackers.

# Boudin Balls

*A mixture of meat, rice, and spices, Boudin is piped into links similar to sausage. A classic appetizer found on many menus and homes in Louisiana is boudin balls like these, which will have your taste buds soaring!*

## Ingredients:

1 lb. boudin
½ cup flour
3 eggs
1 cup bread crumbs
salt and pepper
2 tbsp. parsley
2 tbsp. whole grain mustard
2 tbsp. mayo
1 tbsp. honey
¼ tsp. cayenne pepper
2 green onions
1 cup vegetable oil

## Directions:

1. Remove boudin from casing and add ¼ cup of flour and 1 egg and combine well.

2. Set up a station consisting of 1 plate flour, 1 plate bread crumbs, and a bowl of 2 eggs whisked well.

3. Season flour with salt and pepper.

4. Season bread crumbs with chopped parsley, leaving a bit extra.

5. Mix mustard, mayo, honey, cayenne, green onions, and parsley to make sauce. Set aside.

6. Form boudin into balls and toss lightly with flour, then dredge in egg mixture, and put directly into bread crumbs. Continue to do this until all boudin balls have been made.

7. Heat oil in the skillet to medium-high and add boudin balls. Cook on each side for 2 to 3 minutes until all sides have browned.

8. Sprinkle finished boudin balls with kosher salt.

9. Serve immediately with spicy honey mustard sauce.

# Strawberry, Basil, and Balsamic Crostini

## Ingredients:

1 cup balsamic vinegar
1 tsp. sugar
baguette
2 tbsp. olive oil
1 cup ricotta cheese
cracked pepper
2 cups strawberries, sliced
¼ cup basil, julienned

## Directions:

1. Heat balsamic vinegar and sugar over medium heat in a small pot until vinegar has reduced by half and is thick and syrupy, about 15 to 20 minutes.

2. Heat oven to 400 degrees and brush baguette slices with olive oil and bake for 5 to 10 minutes until toasted.

3. Spread ricotta cheese over top of the crostini, and crack fresh pepper over top.

4. Layer sliced strawberries over top and drizzle with balsamic reduction.

5. Sprinkle with julienned basil and serve immediately.

# Smoky Bacon and Crawfish Flatbread

## Ingredients:

1 cup warm water

1 packet dry yeast

3 tsp. honey

1 tbsp. + 2 tsp. olive oil

2½–¾ cup all-purpose
    flour

1½ tsp. kosher salt

6 slices bacon

½ cup marinara sauce

2 cups mozzarella
    cheese

1 lb. crawfish tails,
    cooked

4 green onions

3 tbsp. parsley

2 ears fresh corn

## Directions:

1. Combine warm water, yeast, and 1 teaspoon honey in a stand mixer bowl. Let the yeast activate for 5 minutes until foamy.

2. Add in 1 tablespoon olive oil, 2 teaspoons honey, and half of the flour and turn the electric mixture on medium with the dough hook attached.

3. Slowly add salt and the rest of the flour until the dough forms a ball and pulls away from the side. Turn the dough out onto a floured surface and knead for a couple of minutes until you have a smooth ball.

4. Place in an oiled bowl and cover with a dish towel and let rise for 30 minutes in a warm area.

5. In the meantime, sauté bacon in a skillet over medium heat until crispy, remove from pan, and set aside.

6. Preheat oven to 400 degrees.

7. After dough has risen, turn out onto the floured surface and punch down. Cut the dough into 4 sections.

8. Roll out each section until each is super thin. Don't roll into a perfect circle; the more rustic the better here.

9. Heat a grill or indoor grill pan to medium-high heat and brush with olive oil. Cut kernels off of corn; set aside.

10. Place each flatbread onto the surface and grill about 2 to 3 minutes per side until dough is cooked and nice grill marks have been made.

11. Remove from the grill and spread a few spoonfuls of marinara sauce onto each flatbread, followed by the cheese, crawfish tails, bacon, and corn.

12. Bake each flatbread for 10 minutes until cheese is bubbly, if grilling indoors. If grilling outdoors, simply layer on toppings and close the grill after lowering the heat until cheese has melted.

13. Top with green onions and parsley before serving.

# Grilled Cajun BBQ Skewers

*Cajun BBQ sauce is not your typical BBQ sauce. It's sweet, spicy, and full of flavor and will be your new favorite sauce for any occasion.*

## Ingredients:

### Cajun BBQ Sauce

1 onion, finely diced
2 garlic cloves, minced
1 tbsp. vegetable oil
½ cup ketchup
1 cup water
¼ cup yellow mustard
3 tbsp. tomato paste
¼ cup worcestershire sauce
1 tsp. Louisiana Hot Sauce
6 tbsp. brown sugar
1 tsp. kosher salt
½ tsp. black pepper
1 tsp. smoked paprika
1 tsp. chili powder
2 tbsp. unsalted butter
½ tsp. cayenne pepper

### Chicken

4 boneless, skinless chicken breasts
olive oil
1½ tsp. salt
1 tsp. cracked black pepper
1 tbsp. fresh parsley, chopped

## Directions:

1. Sauté onions and garlic in vegetable oil over medium heat until tender.
2. Add the rest of the ingredients and bring to a boil.
3. Reduce heat and let simmer for 2 hours until sauce has thickened.
4. Preheat grill to medium heat.
5. Drizzle olive oil over chicken and then season with salt and pepper.
6. Grill the chicken on both sides for 4 to 5 minutes until chicken is cooked through.
7. Baste the chicken with the Cajun BBQ sauce once while cooking.
8. Spoon extra BBQ sauce over the chicken after it's finished cooking, and sprinkle fresh parsley over top.

# Mufalletta Sliders

*The classic muffuletta sandwich is known for layered Italian meats and an olive spread. These tiny takes on that classic creates the perfect party platter!*

## Ingredients:

1 loaf Italian bread
¼ lb. mortadella
¼ lb. ham
½ lb. Genoa salami
¼ lb. Coppa Ham or Capicola
10 slices provolone cheese

### *Olive Spread*

2 cups olives, mix of green
    and kalamata
small jar marinated
    artichokes
½ cup roasted red bell
    peppers
2 green onions
2 garlic cloves
1 stalk celery
2 tsp. dried oregano
1 tbsp. fresh flat leaf parsley
pinch red pepper flakes
2 tbsp. red wine vinegar
½ cup olive oil

## Directions:

1. In a food processor, combine all of the olive spread ingredients and pulse until you have a coarse spread. Set aside.

2. Cut the Italian bread in half and slather the olive spread on both sides of the bread.

3. Layer cheese and meats on entire loaf of bread.

4. Place the top half of the bread onto the layered meats and then slice the sandwich into 3-inch square sliders.

5. Place a toothpick in the center of each slider to prevent the sandwich from coming apart.

6. Serve immediately, chilled or at room temperature.

# Caramelized Bourbon and Thyme Onion Brie Bites

## Ingredients:

1 large white or yellow onion
1 tbsp. olive oil
1 tbsp. unsalted butter
1 tsp. kosher salt
½ tsp. cracked black pepper
1 tbsp. fresh thyme leaves
2 tbsp. bourbon
1 tbsp. brown sugar
frozen mini phyllo cups
4 oz. brie, room temperature

## Directions:

1. Peel onion and then slice into thin rings.

2. Heat olive oil and butter in a large skillet over medium heat.

3. Add onion to the skillet along with salt, pepper, and thyme.

4. Sauté for 20 minutes until onions are browned and caramelized.

5. Add bourbon and brown sugar to the onions and reduce the bourbon slightly.

6. Once bourbon has cooked out for a couple of minutes and brown sugar has melted, turn off the heat. Let the onions cool before assembling the phyllo cups.

7. Dollop a small spoonful of brie in each phyllo cup followed by a teaspoon of the caramelized onions.

8. Bake at 350 degrees for 10 minutes until cheese is bubbly.

9. Serve immediately or at room temperature.

# Baked Cajun Empanadas

## Ingredients:

½ lb. ground beef

½ lb. ground pork

1 tbsp. olive oil

1 onion

½ green bell pepper

1 stalk celery

2 garlic cloves

1 tbsp. fresh parsley

1 tsp. kosher salt

1 tsp. black pepper

½ tsp. Cajun Seasoning
    (see page 3)

1 tbsp. worcestershire sauce

1 tsp. Louisiana Hot Sauce

½ cup beef stock

3 tbsp. flour

12 frozen empanada dough
    discs, room temperature

1 egg + 1 tsp. water

## Directions:

1. Sauté ground meats in olive oil until browned. Remove the meat from the pan.

2. Chop onion, bell pepper, celery, and garlic, into a fine dice. With the parsley, add to the same skillet that the meat was sautéed in and cook until veggies are tender, then season with salt, cracked black pepper, and Cajun Seasoning.

3. Add in Worcestershire sauce and hot sauce and let flavors combine, about 5 more minutes.

4. Make a slurry with the beef stock and flour. Pour into the meat mixture and bring to a boil, then reduce the heat slightly to let the sauce thicken. Remove from heat and let cool.

5. Preheat oven to 400 degrees.

6. Slighty roll out empanada discs on a clean surface and fill each one with 2 tablespoons of the meat mixture.

7. Beat egg and brush edges of the dough before folding one side of the dough over to create a pocket. Press edges with a fork to seal.

8. Place filled empanadas onto a parchment-lined baking sheet and brush tops of the dough with more egg wash to ensure browning.

9. Bake for 15 to 20 minutes until dough has cooked and is golden in color. Serve immediately.

# STATE OF CELEBRATION

You can always find something fun to do in Louisiana. Festivals, concerts, and parades happen throughout the year, and natives know how to celebrate. From the Petroleum and Shrimp Festival, to the Jazz and Heritage Festival, St. Patty's Day parades, and of course Mardi Gras, you'll never find a time when there isn't something exciting to do.

The anticipation for Mardi Gras season starts immediately after the winter holidays come to a close. Mardi Gras parades run on a schedule for a couple weeks in various cities throughout Louisiana. Evidence of the season is made known with colorful beads stuck in oak trees and streets lined with last night's treasures. Droves of visitors and natives alike come out to partake in the festivities. Locals work on stunning floats for months leading up to the parades, creating some of the most extravagant displays you can imagine. With the season comes Mardi Gras Balls, king cakes, and even schools that take a break from the classroom for a few days to be a part of it all.

In addition to Mardi Gras, there are also festivals of all varieties. Strawberry festivals, jambalaya festivals, music festivals, crackling festivals, and so many more. Scattered throughout the state, they are all unique. Most of the festivals are all-day events the whole family can enjoy together.

The amazing food found at any number of these events is half of the draw. I'm not talking about just normal festival and fair food that might be found in other states. Here, you can find Cajun food of all varieties including po' boys, bowls of jambalaya, sausages galore, and anything else your taste buds desire. The pride that Cajuns take in their cooking is no different at a fair or festival than in the kitchen of someone's home. You could (and should) try everything your stomach can handle if attending any of these events.

Louisiana has chosen to create celebrations out of the food and culture that have been around for decades. By embracing local foods like strawberries and rice, and music like jazz, the state has mastered the art of celebrating in a way that no other place does.

# Rosemary Parmesan Pork Rinds

## Ingredients:

1 lb. pork skins

4 cups pork lard or
    vegetable oil

1 tsp. kosher salt

1 tsp. cracked black pepper

1 tbsp. fresh rosemary

¼ cup parmesan, grated

## Directions:

1. Place pork skins in a large pot and cover with water.

2. Bring to a boil and let simmer for 1½ hours until the skins are tender.

3. Remove from water and place skins on a cooling rack over a baking sheet and place in the refrigerator for 1 to 2 hours to cool completely.

4. Once the skin has cooled, scrape the extra fat off the skins.

5. Heat oven to 200 degrees and place skins in oven to dehydrate for 8 hours, until skins are dry and brittle.

6. To fry, heat lard or vegetable oil to about 400 degrees.

7. Fry a couple squares of skins at a time until they puff up.

8. Remove skins to paper towels to drain the excess grease off.

9. Combine salt, pepper, chopped rosemary, and parmesan in a small bowl.

10. Sprinkle the rosemary seasoning over top of the warm pork rinds and serve immediately.

# Cajun Pigs in a Blanket with a Tangy Mustard Brown Sugar Dipping Sauce

## Ingredients:

1 puff pastry sheet
1 tsp. flour
1 lb. andouille sausage
1 egg + 1 tsp. water
1 tbsp. poppy seeds
4 tbsp. whole grain mustard
1 tbsp. brown sugar
1 tsp. apple cider vinegar

## Directions:

1. Preheat oven to 400 degrees.
2. Roll out thawed puff pastry sheet on a lightly floured surface.
3. Cut vertical strips in the puff pastry about 2 inches wide, across the entire piece of dough, and then cut those strips in half once more. You will have 4 (12-inch) strips of puff pastry.
4. Slice andouille sausage at an angle in 12 pieces.
5. Beat egg and water in a small bowl and brush on one end of each strip of puff pastry with the egg wash.
6. Place a piece of cut andouille sausage in the middle of each strip of puff pastry.
7. Fold over the non-egg washed side first, then fold the egg-washed side over on top and press to seal.
8. Brush the tops of each pig in a blanket with more of the egg wash and sprinkle poppy seeds over top of each one.
9. Bake for 15 minutes or until puff pastry is golden brown.
10. While the sausages cook, whisk mustard, brown sugar, and vinegar together in a small saucepan and heat slightly to melt the brown sugar. Place in a small bowl to serve alongside the pigs in a blanket.

# Sweet Tooth

# Satsuma Bundt Cake

## Ingredients:

### *Cake*

3 cups cake flour

1 tsp. salt

½ tsp. baking powder

½ tsp. baking soda

½ cup unsalted butter,
    room temperature

2 cups granulated sugar

4 large eggs, room
    temperature

2 tsp. pure vanilla extract

½ cup satsuma juice (or
    other mandarin)

1 cup buttermilk, room
    temperature

### *Satsuma Syrup*

½ cup granulated sugar

½ cup satsuma juice

### *Satsuma Glaze*

1 cup powdered sugar

2 tbsp. satsuma juice

## Directions:

1. Preheat oven to 350 degrees.

2. Grease a Bundt pan really well by coating every inch with butter and then sprinkling flour on top of the butter. Shake out pan to remove excess flour.

3. Whisk together cake flour, salt, baking powder, and baking soda in a large bowl.

4. With a hand or stand electric mixer, beat butter until smooth and creamy.

5. Add sugar and beat for another couple of minutes until the butter has combined well with the sugar.

6. Add eggs and vanilla, and continue to beat on medium speed until well mixed.

7. Add the satsuma juice and buttermilk and continue to mix.

8. At this time, reduce the speed to low and slowly combine the dry ingredients a little at a time until all is combined, being careful to not overmix.

9. Pour batter into your Bundt pan and bake for 40 to 50 minutes. Allow to cool for 10 minutes. (Test doneness by inserting a toothpick in the center of the cake, ensuring the toothpick is clean after it is pulled back out.)

10. Make the syrup by combining the sugar and satsuma juice in a pot on the stove and heating on medium heat until sugar has dissolved. Turn off heat and set aside.

11. Turn out Bundt cake very carefully onto a wire rack over a plate or parchment paper.

12. Pour the satsuma syrup over top of the cake and continue to let cool completely.

13. After the cake has cooled, make the satsuma glaze by whisking powdered sugar and satsuma juice together and drizzle over the top of the cake.

14. Transfer carefully to a cake plate and serve immediately or cover and store for up to three days.

# *Cafe au Lait* Double Chocolate Chip Ice Cream Sandwiches

*For this recipe, I use an ice cream maker. If you don't have an ice cream machine, you can simply place ice cream into an airtight container and freeze, stirring every hour until ice cream thickens.*

## Ingredients:

### Ice Cream

1½ cups whole milk

2 tbsp. chicory coffee grounds

1 cup sugar

3 egg yolks

2 cups heavy whipping cream

### Cookies

1 cup all-purpose flour

½ cup unsweetened cocoa
    powder

½ tsp. baking soda

¼ tsp. salt

½ cup butter, softened

½ cup brown sugar

½ cup sugar

1 large egg

1 tsp. vanilla extract

¾ cup dark chocolate chips

sea salt to sprinkle on top

## Directions:

### Ice Cream

1. Combine milk, coffee grounds, and sugar, over medium heat, whisking until the sugar dissolves and milk is heated through, but not boiling.

2. Separate the egg whites from their yolks. In a separate bowl, whisk together the egg yolks.

3. Once sugar is dissolved, put a tablespoon at a time of the milk base into the egg yolks until they are tempered (which means bringing the temperature up so the eggs don't scramble).

4. After adding a few tablespoons of the milk to the yolks, add the tempered yolks into the ice cream base. Continue stirring the ice cream base until it thickens slightly, and the back of a wooden spoon is coated. Run a finger down the back of the spoon to ensure the mixture is thick enough.

5. In an airtight container, pour heavy whipping cream, and add the thickened ice cream base.

6. Stir well, seal the container, and refrigerate overnight (or a minimum of 4 hours).

7. Add ice cream base to an ice cream machine and let churn for 30 minutes or until thickened to desired consistency.

8. Once ice cream has thickened, place back in airtight container and freeze overnight.

## Cookies

1. Preheat oven to 350 degrees.
2. In a large bowl, sift together flour, cocoa, baking soda, and salt.
3. In another bowl, beat butter and sugars together until they are fluffy.
4. Add egg and vanilla to the sugars and continue to beat until thoroughly combined.
5. Add dry ingredients a little at a time until all is combined. A wooden spoon works best here, as the batter will be thick.
6. Fold chocolate chips into the batter. Refrigerate the dough for 30 minutes.
7. Drop a tablespoon of the dough onto a parchment or silpat-lined cookie sheet. Sprinkle with sea salt.
8. Bake for 8 to 10 minutes until cookies just set. Let the cookies rest for 5 minutes and then transfer to a cooling rack.

*After your ice cream has frozen overnight, place 1 scoop of ice cream between 2 cookies and press lightly. Serve immediately or freeze the sandwiches by wrapping in parchment paper and then aluminum foil to serve at a later time.

# *Gateau de Sirop* Cupcakes

*Gateau de sirop is a classic cane syrup cake that has been made in Louisiana dating back generations.*

## Ingredients:

2½ cups flour
2½ tsp. ground ginger
2 tsp. cinnamon
¼ tsp. ground cloves
½ nutmeg
½ tsp. salt
1 tsp. baking powder
1½ tsp. baking soda, dissolved in 1 cup
    boiling water
1½ cups pure cane syrup
½ cup vegetable oil
1 egg, beaten

### *Cinnamon Cream Cheese Frosting*

8 oz. cream cheese, room temperature
¼ cup butter, room temperature
2 cups powdered sugar
2 tsp. cinnamon + more for dusting
¼ tsp. salt
2 tbsp. milk

## Directions:

1. Preheat oven to 350 degrees.
2. In a large bowl, whisk together flour, ginger, cinnamon, cloves, nutmeg, salt, and baking powder.
3. In another large bowl, combine cane syrup, vegetable oil, and egg, and mix well.
4. Slowly add one-third of the flour mixture at a time followed by one-third of the baking soda mixture at a time, until all ingredients are combined and smooth.
5. Line a cupcake pan with cupcake liners and pour batter inside each liner.
6. Bake for 30 minutes until cupcakes are done and a toothpick comes out clean. Let cupcakes cool completely on a cooling rack.
7. In a stand mixer or other mixing bowl, beat cream cheese and butter until creamy, then slowly add in powdered sugar, cinnnamon, and salt.
8. Add in milk, 1 tablespoon at a time, until desired consistency has been reached.
9. Frost cupcakes and dust with extra cinnamon.

# THE SWEET SPOT

I have had a sweet tooth for as long as I can remember. I get this quality from my mom, who, for most of my life growing up, always ended her day with a small bowl of vanilla ice cream. I am one of those people who need (or want) a little bite of something sweet after almost every meal. It's to my detriment, but I can't help myself. Ice cream is my number one vice, but I most definitely do not discriminate when it comes to dessert.

After moving to Louisiana, I was introduced to a whole new world of desserts I had been deprived of my whole life. One bite of a fluffy beignet covered with powdered sugar, a spoonful of bread pudding swimming in a bourbon sauce, a piece of a king cake, and a handful of pralines made to perfection, and I knew that Louisiana and I were going to be fast friends. My sweet tooth would be satisfied here and would probably never be the same again.

After the holidays, as part of the pre-Lenten celebrations of Mardi Gras and Carnival season, comes the release of the famous king cake. It's my favorite sweet treat from Louisiana and, since they are only available for a short period of time, I have to eat as much of them as I can before the season is over! During Mardi Gras season, king cakes become part of every gathering, work place, and home environment, and then disappear almost as quickly as they came after Fat Tuesday. King cakes are a quintessential Louisiana dessert and a huge part of Mardi Gras tradition! I prefer the plain cinnamon or cream cheese flavors, but king cakes are offered in a multitude of flavor combinations from pecan praline to strawberry. Placed inside is a plastic baby, and those who get the baby in their piece of cake are thought to have luck and prosperity. That's reason enough to partake in the tradition, if you ask me.

While we are on the subject of luck, you can consider yourself lucky if you ever have tasted beignets from Cafe du Monde! These beignets paired with a cup of hot and creamy *café au lait* while sitting in the middle of the French Quarter is an experience that everyone should have. And if you don't leave with a little powdered sugar on your face or your shirt, then you didn't do it right.

Is visiting Louisiana going to be good for your waistline? Probably not, but I can guarantee every single bite will be worth it. With so many options for decadent treats in Louisiana, you really can't go wrong. There are plenty of options to satisfy even your sweet tooth's sweet tooth!

You can find my own takes on these classic desserts right here. My take on classic Louisiana desserts can be done right in your kitchen and will have your taste buds transported to somewhere down on the bayou!

# Creole Sweet Heat Brownie Parfaits with Vanilla Bean Whipped Cream

## Ingredients:

### *Creole Sweet Heat Brownies*

3 oz. semisweet chocolate, roughly chopped

1 stick unsalted butter

1⅓ cup granulated sugar

2 eggs

1 tsp. vanilla extract

2 tbsp. brewed chicory coffee

¼ tsp. cayenne

½ tsp. cinnamon + extra for dusting

½ tsp. sea salt

⅔ cup all-purpose flour

### *Vanilla Bean Whipped Cream*

1 vanilla bean, or 1 tsp. vanilla extract

1 cup heavy whipping cream

2 tbsp. powdered sugar

## Directions:

1. Preheat oven to 350 degrees and line an 8 x 8 square baking pan with parchment paper, or grease well.

2. In a double boiler, heat chocolate and butter until butter is just melted.

3. Remove from heat and stir to combine.

4. Whisk in sugar, eggs one at a time, vanilla, coffee, cayenne pepper, cinnamon, and salt.

5. Slowly fold in flour until just combined.

6. Pour batter into baking pan and bake for 25 to 30 minutes until a toothpick inserted comes out clean.

7. Let cool completely and then refrigerate for 20 minutes.

8. Remove brownies from the refrigerator and cut into small 1-inch squares.

9. Take a small knife and run it down the center of the vanilla bean and then scrape out the seeds inside.

10. In a stainless steel bowl, combine whipping cream, powdered sugar, and vanilla beans, and whip on medium-high speed until stiff peaks have formed.

11. Layer squares of brownie with your fresh whipped cream in a glass.

12. Dust with cinnamon and shave extra chocolate over top of each parfait; serve immediately.

# Bourbon Butterscotch Bread Pudding

## Ingredients:

### *Pudding*

1 loaf day-old Italian bread
½ cup heavy cream
1½ cups milk
5 eggs
2 tsp. vanilla extract
½ cup brown sugar
1 cup granulated sugar
¼ cup butter, melted

### *Bourbon Butterscotch Sauce*

3 tbsp. butter
½ cup light corn syrup
1 cup light brown sugar
1 tsp. salt
½ cup heavy cream
2 tbsp. bourbon

## Directions:

1. Preheat oven to 350 degrees.

2. Cube bread, and place in a large bowl.

3. In another bowl, combine heavy cream, milk, eggs, vanilla, brown sugar, granulated sugar, and melted butter, and whisk to combine.

4. Pour mixture over the bread cubes and let sit for 8 to 10 minutes.

5. Grease a 9 x 10 baking dish and pour soaked bread cubes and extra custard filling inside.

6. Bake for 40 to 45 minutes until golden brown and the custard has cooked through.

7. While the pudding is baking, combine butter, corn syrup, brown sugar, and salt in a saucepan over medium-high heat.

8. Bring to a boil, then remove from heat.

9. Stir in heavy cream and bourbon and let cool.

10. To serve, pour the desired amount of sauce over the pudding (warm or at room temperature) and serve with extra sauce on the side.

# Dark Chocolate Toffee Pecan Bars

Ingredients:

### Crust

2 sticks butter
$^2/_3$ cup packed
    brown sugar
$2^2/_3$ cup flour
1 tsp. salt

### Filling

4 eggs
$^3/_4$ cup brown sugar
1 cup light corn syrup
4 tbsp. butter, melted
$1^1/_2$ tsp. vanilla extract
$^1/_2$ cup toffee bits
1 cup dark chocolate chips
$^1/_2$ tsp. salt
2 cups pecans

### Directions:

1. Preheat oven to 350 degrees.

2. To make the crust, beat butter and sugar together until creamy.

3. Add flour and salt and mix until crumbly.

4. Line a baking sheet with aluminum foil, allowing some overhang. Press the crust into the aluminum foil in an even layer.

5. Bake for 20 minutes.

6. For the filling, combine eggs, brown sugar, corn syrup, butter, vanilla, toffee bits, dark chocolate chips, salt, and pecans in a bowl.

7. Pour over hot crust and bake for another 20 minutes.

8. Let cool completely. Remove bars from the baking sheet and slice into bars.

# Bananas Foster Banana Bread

## Ingredients:

2 very ripe bananas, mashed
  (leaving a little chunky)
2 eggs
⅓ cup buttermilk
¼ cup vegetable oil
¼ cup Greek yogurt
1½ tsp. vanilla extract
1 tsp. rum extract or regular
  rum
1½ cups sugar
1¾ cup all-purpose flour
1 tsp. baking soda
½ tsp. kosher salt

### *Bananas Foster Sauce*

½ stick butter
½ cup brown sugar
pinch salt
½ cup water
¼ cup spiced rum
1 banana

## Directions:

1. Preheat oven to 325 degrees.
2. Grease a 9 x 5 loaf pan, or line with parchment paper.
3. Mash bananas, and mix together with the rest of the wet ingredients.
4. Sift together dry ingredients.
5. Slowly fold dry ingredients into the wet ingredients until well combined.
6. Pour batter into your greased or lined loaf pan, and bake for approximately 1 hour and 15 minutes, depending on your oven.
7. To test if the bread is baked through, stick a toothpick in the middle and see if it comes out clean.
8. To make the sauce, melt butter, then add brown sugar, salt, and water, and stir to combine. Let the brown sugar melt and thicken.
9. Once sauce has thickened, turn off heat and carefully pour in the spiced rum, and stir to combine.
10. Slice 1 banana and put into the sauce; stir to coat.
11. Poke holes in the banana bread with a toothpick and then pour sauce over the banana bread. Serve immediately.

# King Cake Ice Cream

*King cake is one of the most well-known desserts in Louisiana, and the classic flavors of cinnamon and cream cheese make for the ultimate homemade ice cream!*

## Ingredients:

### Ice Cream Base

1½ cups whole milk
2 cups granulated
    sugar
3 egg yolks
4 oz. cream cheese
2 cups heavy whipping
    cream

### Cinnamon Swirl

½ cup brown sugar
⅓ cup water
2 tbsp. butter
1½ tsp. cinnamon

## Directions:

1. Combine milk and sugar over medium heat, whisking until the sugar dissolves and milk is heated through, but not boiling. This is your ice cream base.
2. In a separate bowl, whisk together the egg yolks.
3. Once sugar is dissolved, put 1 tablespoon at a time of the ice cream base into the egg yolks until they are tempered (which means bringing the temperature up so the eggs don't scramble).
4. After adding a few tablespoons of the warm milk in with the yolks, add the tempered yolks into the rest of the ice cream base mixture. Continue stirring the ice cream base until the back of a wooden spoon is coated.
5. Strain the ice cream base through a fine mesh strainer into a separate bowl.
6. Cut the cream cheese into small cubes and whisk into the hot ice cream base until melted. (Small bits of cream cheese is fine.)
7. In an airtight container, pour heavy whipping cream, and add the thickened cream cheese ice cream base.
8. Stir well and seal the container and refrigerate overnight, or a minimum of 4 hours.
9. In a small saucepan, add brown sugar, water, butter, and cinnamon, and melt over medium heat.
10. Bring the cinnamon mixture to room temperature, or chill until ready to make ice cream.
11. Follow ice cream maker directions after ice cream base has thoroughly chilled.
12. Once ice cream has thickened, layer the cream cheese ice cream and the cinnamon sugar syrup a layer at a time in an airtight container until you have used up both and freeze overnight.

# Almond Beignet Bites

## Ingredients:

1 packet dry active yeast

3 tbsp. granulated sugar

1 cup warm water

3 cups flour

½ tsp. salt

2 eggs

1 tsp. almond extract

2 quarts + 2 tbsp. vegetable oil

powdered sugar

## Directions:

1. In a stand mixer bowl, combine yeast, 1 tablespoon sugar, and warm water, and let sit for 5 to 10 minutes until yeast is bubbly.

2. In a large bowl, combine flour, 2 tablespoons sugar, and salt.

3. Whisk eggs, almond extract, and 2 tablespoons vegetable oil together and then add into the yeast mixture.

4. With the mixer speed on low, slowly add in the dry ingredients until the dough has come together.

5. Remove and place into an oiled bowl and cover with a dish towel for 1 to 2 hours in the fridge, until dough has doubled in size.

6. Turn the dough out onto a heavily floured surface and knead a few times.

7. Heat vegetable oil over medium high heat until the temperature is at 350 degrees. Test by carefully dropping a small piece of dough inside—when it sizzles, the oil is ready.

8. Pull off bite-sized pieces of the dough and drop into the vegetable oil and cook on each side for about 2 to 3 minutes, until dough is golden brown.

9. Remove from the oil and place onto a paper towel-lined plate or cooling wire rack to let excess grease drain.

10. Dust the cooked beignets liberally with powdered sugar and serve immediately.

# Strawberry Cream Popsicles

*Louisiana strawberries are in season twice a year (November to January, and March to May) and are so sweet you could consider them candy on their own, but blended with cream and sugar, they make for a delicious and refreshing popsicle.*

## Ingredients:

½ cup heavy cream
¼ cup granulated sugar
1 pint strawberries

## Directions:

1. Heat heavy cream and sugar in a small saucepan over medium heat until sugar has dissolved. Let cool slightly.

2. Remove stems from the strawberries and wash the berries.

3. Slice the strawberries in half and purée in a food processor or blender until smooth.

4. Add in the sweetened heavy cream and purée until well combined.

5. Pour the mixture into popsicle molds and freeze overnight.

6. To serve, run under warm water for 30 seconds until popsicle releases from the mold.

# Roasted Sweet Potato Milkshakes

## Ingredients:

1 sweet potato
1 tbsp. + 1 tsp. brown sugar
1 tsp. cinnamon
1 tbsp. butter
¼ cup pecans
1 pint vanilla ice cream
¼ cup milk
½ cup heavy whipping cream
2 tbsp. powdered sugar

## Directions:

1. Heat oven to 450 degrees.
2. Cut sweet potato in half and sprinkle with 1 teaspoon of brown sugar. Roast for 45 minutes or until sweet potato is tender. Let cool.
3. Combine 1 tablespoon brown sugar, cinnamon, and butter in a small saucepan over medium heat and cook until sugar and butter have melted.
4. Add pecans to the pan and stir to coat. Set aside and let cool.
5. Scoop the inside of the sweet potato out, discarding the skins.
6. Combine vanilla ice cream, sweet potato flesh, and milk in a blender and combine until smooth and creamy.
7. Combine whipping cream and powdered sugar and whip until thickened.
8. To serve, divide the sweet potato ice cream mixture into 2 glasses, top with whipped cream, and pour the pecan brown sugar mixture over top.

# Happy Hour

# Pimm's Cup

*Nothing is more refreshing in the summertime than a Pimm's cup. This quintessential cocktail of Louisiana boasts refreshing cucumber and lemon as the primary flavor notes.*

### Ingredients:

juice from 1 lemon
4 oz. pimm's liquor
ginger ale
cucumber slices
lemon slices

### Directions:

1. Fill glass with crushed ice.
2. Squeeze half of the lemon juice per glass.
3. Add 2 oz. of Pimm's liquor to each glass.
4. Top with ginger ale.
5. Garnish with cucumber slices and lemon slices.

# Meyer Lemon Thyme Crush

### Ingredients:

½ cup sugar
½ cup water
4 sprigs of thyme, plus extra for garnish
juice from 4 meyer lemons, about ½ cup (can
    substitute regular lemons)
4 oz. vodka
club soda for topping

### Directions:

1. In a small saucepan, make a thyme simple syrup by combining sugar and water and bring to a boil. Add thyme sprigs and turn off heat. Let sit for 5 minutes.

2. Strain the thyme simple syrup and chill thoroughly.

3. Combine lemon juice, vodka, and 2 tablespoons of the thyme simple syrup.

4. Shake and pour over crushed ice.

5. Top off the cocktail with club soda and garnish with extra lemon slices and thyme sprigs.

# Blackberry Gin Fizz

**Ingredients:**

¼ cup blackberries

1 oz. lemon juice

1 oz. lime juice

1 egg white

1 oz. heavy cream, or half-
   and-half

ice cubes

1 oz. gin

soda water for topping

**Directions:**

1. Muddle blackberries and strain the juice into a cocktail shaker.

2. Add lemon juice, lime juice, egg white, heavy cream, ice cubes, and gin, and shake 100 times until the egg white is frothy.

3. Pour into a cocktail glass and top off with soda water. Serve immediately.

# Satsuma Sage Mule

*Satsumas are my favorite of the citrus varieties grown in Louisiana. They taste similar to a mandarin, but slightly sweeter, making them perfect for cocktails of all varieties.*

## Ingredients:

8 sage leaves + more for garnish
1 cup fresh satsuma juice
  (or clementine juice)
2 oz. vodka
1 ginger beer

## Directions:

1. Muddle sage leaves in the satsuma juice in the bottom of a cocktail shaker until flavors are released.
2. Add vodka to the juice, along with a couple of ice cubes, and shake vigorously until chilled.
3. Pour satsuma sage mule over ice and top off with ginger beer.
4. Serve immediately and garnish with extra sage leaves and satsuma slices.

# Spiced Pear Sangria

## Ingredients:

1 bottle cabernet sauvignon red wine
¼ cup brandy
juice from 1 lemon
2 sliced pears
1 lemon, sliced

### Spiced Simple Syrup

½ cup sugar
½ cup water
2 cinnamon sticks
1 star anise
10 whole cloves

## Directions:

1. Make simple syrup by combining sugar, water, cinnamon sticks, star anise, and cloves in a small saucepan and bring to a boil. Turn off heat and let sit for 10 minutes.

2. Strain the simple syrup.

3. Combine wine, brandy, simple syrup, lemon juice, sliced pears, and sliced lemons in a large pitcher.

4. Chill thoroughly overnight to let flavors combine.

5. Serve the next day over ice with extra slices of pears and lemons for garnish.

# A SPIRITED STATE OF MIND

Cocktails have taken on their own culinary excellence. The classics like gin and tonic, whiskey sours, and vodka martinis still exist, but the new age of cocktails have me more excited than ever. With endless possibilities, cocktails are one of my favorite ways to express myself in the kitchen.

In Louisiana, the same rings true, maybe even more so. As people who pride themselves on the fact that they know how to have a good time, cocktails are at the center of every gathering just as much as the food is. On top of that, you'll find an endless supply of fantastic watering holes where you can drink to your heart's content.

New Orleans is one of my favorite cities to explore local bars and eateries featuring signature cocktails that make your taste buds swoon. Walking down streets lined with beautiful Spanish-inspired architecture, you'll discover a neighborhood bar, a hotel lounge, or a swanky upscale establishment where you can find the classic and new age cocktails Louisiana is known for.

While on Bourbon Street, I would suggest sipping on a hurricane daiquiri while soaking in the sights around you. With a drink in hand, you can explore local shops, art galleries, and street entertainment throughout the entire city.

For a different feel, try walking down my favorite street, St. Charles, and stopping in at The Columns Hotel. They have a bar downstairs that serves up all the classics including Ramos Gin Fizzes and Sazeracs. From there, I would suggest hopping onto the street car and hitting up a dinner spot nearby.

Old world charm, gorgeous architecture, and fabulous food and drinks galore are just a few reasons why New Orleans is one of my favorite cities. Louisiana happens to believe that drinking is appropriate starting with breakfast, and brunch happens to be the one of the best ways to get the weekend started. Who wouldn't want to indulge in a spicy Creole Bloody Mary to kickstart any Saturday or Sunday? In more cases than not, natives will always find a good reason for cocktails to become a part of any equation.

There is a magical quality to New Orleans incomparable to any other place that I have visited. The people are friendly, proud of where they come from, and the city is a mix of all ethnicities. The cocktails mimic this quality in that they are just as eclectic and are a very important part of the culture.

# Rosemary Grapefruit French Gimlet

## Ingredients:

1 grapefruit
1 oz. St. Germain
1 oz. gin
1 sprig rosemary

## Directions:

1. Juice grapefruit.
2. Combine grapefruit juice, St. Germain, gin, and one sprig of rosemary in a cocktail shaker.
3. Muddle the rosemary sprig to release the flavors of the herb.
4. Add a few ice cubes and shake the cocktail until chilled thoroughly.
5. Strain into a cocktail glass and serve immediately.

# Mango Bourbon Smash

## Ingredients:

1 mango
¼ cup fresh lime juice
2 oz. bourbon
ginger ale

## Directions:

1. Cut up mango and purée with lime juice until smooth.

2. Spoon 2 tablespoons of the mango lime purée into each cocktail glass.

3. Pour 1 ounce of bourbon into each glass.

4. Top off each glass with ginger ale and stir to combine.

5. Serve immediately.

# Grilled Pineapple Vanilla Daiquiri

**Ingredients:**

½ pineapple
¼ cup fresh lime juice
1 tsp. vanilla
½ cup rum
1 cup ice
¼ cup Simple Syrup
  (see page 3)

**Directions:**

1. Heat grill to medium heat, around 350 degrees.

2. Cut pineapple into strips and grill on each side for 2 to 3 minutes, just charring the outside but not cooking the inside.

3. Remove the pineapple from the heat and let cool.

4. In a blender, combine the grilled pineapple, lime juice, vanilla, rum, ice, and Simple Syrup, and blend until smooth.

5. Pour into cocktail glasses and serve immediately.

# Strawberry Mojitos

## Ingredients:

4 strawberries, stems removed and cut in half
10 fresh mint leaves
2 tbsp. sugar
juice from 2 limes (about ¼ cup)
3 oz. clear rum
ice cubes
soda water for topping
lime wedges, strawberries, and mint, to garnish

## Directions:

1. Purée your strawberries, mint leaves, sugar, and lime juice together.
2. Strain the liquid with a fine mesh strainer into a separate glass.
3. In a cocktail shaker, combine your strained strawberry purée, rum, and a couple of ice cubes, and give it a good shake.
4. Pour into two cocktail glasses filled with ice.
5. Top off glass with soda water.
6. Garnish with fresh lime wedges, strawberries, and mint leaves. Serve immediately.

# Sparkling Blueberry Basil Lemonade

## Ingredients:

¼ cup blueberries
2 lemons, juiced
5 leaves fresh basil
2 tbsp. Simple Syrup, (see page 3)
crushed ice
prosecco
blueberries, lemons, and basil, to garnish

## Directions:

1.  Smash blueberries, lemon juice, basil leaves, and Simple Syrup in the bottom of glass.

2.  Add crushed ice.

3.  Top with prosecco.

4.  Garnish with blueberries, lemon wedges, and a fresh basil leaf.

# Creole Bloody Mary

## Ingredients:

2 cups low-sodium spicy tomato juice
2 tbsp. horseradish
1 tsp. Louisiana Hot Sauce
½ tsp. salt
½ tsp. pepper
½ tsp. steak seasoning
1 tsp. olive juice
juice from 1 lemon
juice from 1 lime
1 tbsp. worcestershire sauce
¼ cup vodka
vegetables for garnish, such as pickled okra,
    lemon wedges, and olives.

## Directions:

1. In a pitcher, mix all ingredients together and stir well.
2. Fill glasses with ice and pour Bloody Mary mixture over top.

# Cherry French 75

## Ingredients:

½ cup sugar
½ cup water
¼ cup Bing cherries
2 oz. gin
squeeze of fresh lemon juice
ice cubes
prosecco
lemon peel and cherries, to
    garnish

## Directions:

1. Make a cherry simple syrup by combining sugar, water, and pitted cherries in a small saucepan and bring to a boil. Let sit for 15 minutes, strain, and chill thoroughly.

2. In a cocktail shaker, combine cherry simple syrup, gin, and lemon juice with a couple of ice cubes. Shake for a few seconds.

3. Pour into two cocktail glasses and top off with prosecco.

4. Garnish with lemon peel and a fresh cherry.

# Acknowledgments

First and foremost, I would like to thank my mom for instilling in me my love of food and teaching me the ins and outs of the kitchen. You taught me that through food, you can find common ground with anyone!

I would also like to thank my in-laws for welcoming me into their Cajun family with open arms and allowing me to be submerged in a culture that I have grown to love so deeply. I will forever call Louisiana my second home.

Lastly, I would like to thank my husband, Canean, without whom this book would not have been possible. Thank you for taking care of our newborn baby while I spent hours in the kitchen, thank you for washing dishes, thank you for telling me I could do this when I had moments of doubt, and thank you for loving me through it all!

Xo

# Conversion Charts

## OVEN TEMPERATURES

| Fahrenheit | Celsius | Gas Mark |
|---|---|---|
| 225° | 110° | $\frac{1}{4}$ |
| 250° | 120° | $\frac{1}{2}$ |
| 275° | 140° | 1 |
| 300° | 150° | 2 |
| 325° | 160° | 3 |
| 350° | 180° | 4 |
| 375° | 190° | 5 |
| 400° | 200° | 6 |
| 425° | 220° | 7 |
| 450° | 230° | 8 |

# METRIC AND IMPERIAL CONVERSIONS
## (THESE CONVERSIONS ARE ROUNDED FOR CONVENIENCE)

| Ingredient | Cups/Tablespoons/Teaspoons | Ounces | Grams/Milliliters |
|---|---|---|---|
| Butter | 1 cup=16 tablespoons= 2 sticks | 8 ounces | 230 grams |
| Cream cheese | 1 tablespoon | 0.5 ounce | 14.5 grams |
| Cheese, shredded | 1 cup | 4 ounces | 110 grams |
| Cornstarch | 1 tablespoon | 0.3 ounce | 8 grams |
| Flour, all-purpose | 1 cup/1 tablespoon | 4.5 ounces/0.3 ounce | 125 grams/8 grams |
| Flour, whole wheat | 1 cup | 4 ounces | 120 grams |
| Fruit, dried | 1 cup | 4 ounces | 120 grams |
| Fruits or veggies, chopped | 1 cup | 5 to 7 ounces | 145 to 200 grams |
| Fruits or veggies, puréed | 1 cup | 8.5 ounces | 245 grams |
| Honey, maple syrup, or corn syrup | 1 tablespoon | .75 ounce | 20 grams |
| Liquids: cream, milk, water, or juice | 1 cup | 8 fluid ounces | 240 milliliters |
| Oats | 1 cup | 5.5 ounces | 150 grams |
| Salt | 1 teaspoon | 0.2 ounce | 6 grams |
| Spices: cinnamon, cloves, ginger, or nutmeg (ground) | 1 teaspoon | 0.2 ounce | 5 milliliters |
| Sugar, brown, firmly packed | 1 cup | 7 ounces | 200 grams |
| Sugar, white | 1 cup/1 tablespoon | 7 ounces/0.5 ounce | 200 grams/12.5 grams |
| Vanilla extract | 1 teaspoon | 0.2 ounce | 4 grams |

# Index